A CRY OF THE HEART

Human Trafficking - One Survivor's True Story

Debra Rush

with Penelope Childers

Cover designed by EA Books

Debra Rush with Penelope Childers
www.btcfresno.org

Printed in the United States of America

First Printing: Mar 2019
EA Books

ISBN-13 978-1-9459762-1-6

PRAISE FOR
A CRY OF THE HEART

"Heart-wrenching, courageously transparent, fast-paced, and inspiring story of a survivor who becomes a victor and ultimately a warrior in the battle against sex trafficking. The hand of God is on Debra from the beginning."

—Francine Rivers,
New York Times, best-selling author

"*A Cry of the Heart* is one of those unforgettable books about the most heartbreaking of topics—sexual trafficking. We know it happens, but we don't know those who it happens to. This book is that missing piece of the puzzle, and it takes us behind the scenes of this dark and evil practice through the eyes of Debra, a young woman forced into a life she never wanted or dreamed of. But that's not the end of her story. As her healing journey began, she is determined to reach back and help others out of a terrible life they never wanted or dreamed of, either. Read this book and you'll never forget."

—Susy Flory,
New York Times author or co-author of 14 books
and director of the West Coast Christian Writers Conference

"Deserted by her mother as a baby, Debra doesn't see her mother again until she is five. At the age of eleven, Debra spends the night with her mom—in prison. Even when her mother is free, men and drugs take preference over Debra. Her father tries to raise her well, and so does her grandma, but they aren't mom. And mom is the one Debra longs for. Dad is church and rules and such. Mom is men and drugs and excitement. So, Debra follows in mom's broken footsteps, all the way to selling herself on the street. But when she sees a video on sex trafficking, Debra finally manages to pick up the shards of her broken past and piece them together. She is a victim, just like her mother. But Debra is not like her mother. She is determined to break the chains that bind her, and to make a way of escape for others trapped on the streets. *A Cry of the Heart* will make you laugh, and it will make you cry. It will touch your heart, and then break it. Most of all, it will change you forever."

—Kay Marshall Strom,
Author of over 42 books, most recently on social issues

"*A Cry of the Heart* by Debra Rush is a riveting story of pain and degradation, of suffering and sorrow—but also of hope and redemption. Readers will follow Debra's story into the darkest places imaginable, then find their way out again as the light of God's love reaches out to Debra's heart and brings healing to her wounded soul. A tough read, but well worth the emotional investment!"

—Kathi Macias (www.kathimacias.com)
Award-winning author of more than fifty books, including* Deliver Me from Evil, *the first in her fictional human-trafficking "Deliverance" series

"Debra Rush and Penelope Childers take the reader into the shadowy and perverse world of sex trafficking and into the light where chains are broken, and lives are set free. *A Cry of the Heart* discloses a message of truth in the world of darkness."

—Victoria Pitts Caine
***Award winning author of* Alvarado Gold *and* The Tempering Agent**

"Penelope Childers captures the voice of this amazing woman and her phoenix-type rising out of trafficking. Riveting and informative testimony, yet tastefully revealed."

—Julie B. Cosgrove
Award-winning author of the trafficking suspense trilogy
Hush in the Storm, Legitimate Lies, *and Freed to Forgive*

"Debra Rush provides you first-hand insight into the underworld that is human trafficking. As a second-generation victim of this horrible crime, she provides a realistic and unique perspective of how young, innocent girls can get tricked into this life, and the violence that becomes their reality. She is raw, honest about her own experience as a trafficking victim, and incredibly articulate in describing the otherwise unbelievable hold that traffickers attain over their victims. For anyone interested in the truth about Human Trafficking, this book is for you."

—Lisa Smittcamp
Fresno County District Attorney

"Debra Rush came to the Fresno Rescue Mission out of her need for help and recovery. Over the time I have known her I have watched her grow spiritually and emotionally, coming to a place of healing in her own life and heart. She is a woman God has filled with passion and empathy for those who need help in becoming healed and made whole. I have had the opportunity to mentor her in her ministry of Breaking the Chains and had the privilege of seeing God's work in her life. She is one of those God has touched in a very powerful way, using her brokenness to bring wholeness to others."

—Don Eskes
Former CEO, Fresno Rescue Mission

Dedicated to survivors of sex trafficking
and those waiting to be rescued.

A Cry of the Heart is a true story.
Several names have been changed. Some story detail and conversations have been recreated from memory and author's creativity.

My story may be hard for some to read. There are times when you might not like me. Honestly, there were times that I did not like myself. It is my hope that you will find the self-forgiveness and the ability to forgive those who have harmed you that I have found.

FOREWORD

A silent plague runs rampant in our cities as it does throughout most of the world. It was once called prostitution, but it is now recognized as human trafficking or sex trafficking. It involves the entrapment, imprisonment, and sale of young girls (and sometimes boys) and women for sex. No one is immune. It's a crime that has existed and been misunderstood for decades.

Fresno, California has a population of over 500,000. After twenty-one years with the Fresno police department, I was sworn in as the Chief of Police on August 1, 2001. The general feeling by most of the community and society at that time, including law enforcement, was that women sold themselves for sex as a matter of choice. My thinking was no different until 2010, when members of my law enforcement team convinced me something very sinister was going on in our city. Maybe women who walked the streets, selling themselves, didn't have a choice—maybe they were the victims, not the criminals. Sergeant Curt Chastain and detectives from our Vice Intelligence Unit brought me clear and compelling evidence that young, innocent teenage girls are lured, by gang members, into a lifestyle that was portrayed to them as glamorous. Oftentimes, runaways and unsupervised girls are sought out on social media. Girls who are insecure, unloved, and starved for affection are perfect targets. These gang members—pimps—are pros at drawing innocent girls in.

A pimp targets a girl, treats her like she is truly special, and gives her his undivided attention. Maybe for the first time in her life, she feels loved. But it is only a matter of time before she is asked to perform sex acts for others as a demonstration of either her love or loyalty to her "man" who becomes her pimp. If she refuses, the girl will endure repeated physical beatings until she will have no choice but to conform and perform.

Once caught in the snare, it is difficult to get out. The brainwashing that transpires over a period time and the feeling of hopelessness converts these females into believing they are selling themselves of their own free will. Victim or criminal? The answer became obvious.

In the fall of 2014, I received a call from a friend, Tom Sommers, who wanted me to meet Debra Woods. She requested that I speak at the initial fundraiser for her new nonprofit, Breaking the Chains, an organization founded to rescue and rehabilitate women from sex trafficking. I don't usually accept invitations to speak at nonprofit events, but the timing was right, and this subject had piqued my interest dramatically over the last several years. My initial response was a chuckle, but I told Tom to have her call my office and make an appointment.

By the time Debra called, much progress had been made in dealing with pimps and gang members, but there was no place for the victims to go. They did not fit the government funded definition of those who most organizations could assist. Many wanted to help, but their hands were tied.

I was curious about Debra, who wanted to specifically help victims of sex trafficking. We met in my office in early 2015. She brought the Breaking the Chains co-founder, Tiffany Apodaca. Several members of the vice squad attended the meeting including Sergeant Chastain. We listened as Debra poured out her heart and told us her story of how God had saved her and her desire and plan to help those she left behind. Listening to Debra and seeing the pain in her eyes, helped me more fully realize the trauma sex traffic victims endure.

I agreed I would help, including speaking at her banquet. It was obvious to those of us in the room that Debra had the passion, courage and vision we desperately needed in our fight to battle sex trafficking in our city. Thanks to stories such as Debra's, the operating philosophy of the Fresno Police Department is much different than it was prior to 2010. We now see these girls for who they are—victims. Breaking the Chains works closely with members of the Fresno Police Department and serves as a valuable resource to our vice detectives. Breaking the Chains has enjoyed an amazing outpouring of community support.

Sadly, not all victims find the strength to disclose the life they were subjected to as Debra has. However, if we can get just one young girl rescued and convince her to tell her story, we can save multiple victims. Conservatively, every trafficker controls at least ten girls. So, if we can remove just fifty traffickers from society, we can free 500 victims.

Sex trafficking has replaced the illegal drug trade as the main source of income for gangs. Instead of getting more drugs to sell, they have realized they can resell the human trafficking victim over and over again. This is a cycle that must be broken, and it can be. It all begins with the awareness that the next victim could be someone you know.

Debra's story reinforced my belief in the human spirit. What she has overcome and accomplished, with God as her guide, is truly inspirational. Not only did I say "yes" to speaking at the 2015 banquet, but I have spoken at every Breaking the Chains banquet since. Debra Rush is my friend, whom I'm proud to know. I am honored to serve on the board of Breaking the Chains. Debra's passion for rescuing victims from a life of human trafficking is contagious and shines throughout her story.

Read *A Cry of the Heart* and follow Debra on her journey from victim to rescuer, from hopelessness to hope, from pretend love to finding real love, and to 2018 California State Woman of the Year. You won't forget Debra Rush. Her story might even change your life.

Chief Jerry Dyer
Safety, Service, Trust
Chief of Police, Fresno, California

CRY OF THE HEART

Love is conditional.
Love comes with expectation.
Love is based on performance.
Love is a competition.
Love has limits.
Love requires gratification.
Love is physical.
Love offers no protection.
Love hurts.
Love is not my redemption.
Please tell me I am wrong.
Please show me this is not true.
Hold me close in your arms and tell me what to do.
Everyone's arms come with conditions.
A price I do not want to pay,
I long for something different,
A hope for a new day.
My heart is on fire.
It burns for the truth.
My mind is spinning.
Please help,
I am waiting on you.

Debra Woods

This poem was written at a time when I hated who I'd become. A time when there seemed to be no help for someone who had lived the life I had. Someone who had been tricked, trafficked, and knew the world of pimps and prostitution from the inside out. Someone who believed her redemption to be impossible. This poem was written at a time when *hope* was an empty word.

PROLOGUE

October 2010
Pinecrest Christian Conference Center
San Bernardino Mountains—Southern California

The fresh scent of pine-filled air caught my breath as I stepped out of the car. I looked forward to a weekend where I could forget about my worries—especially my past. The eight women who were with me knew my secrets, but others would see me as just another Christian woman.

At least I hoped they would.

My blue jeans and a pink, zip-up sweatshirt covered my tattoos. My thick, brown hair, pulled back in a ponytail, made me feel as if I fit in.

Excitement bubbled in my chest as I engaged with the women I met at Pinecrest. They seemed as happy to meet me as I was to meet them. I flashed a bright smile and looked them in the eyes as I introduced myself. Some were young mothers like me. Others were older, perhaps grandmothers. I loved making these new friends, but purposely kept my conversations in the now, so they wouldn't figure out my past. As I watched them laugh and hug each other, I wondered what they would think if they knew.

Tables were laid out on either side of the walkway that led to the various meeting rooms. Each table previewed the workshops offered the following day. At the last display, I stopped. A poster of a young woman caught my attention. The girl leaned into the window of a late-model sports car, talking to a man. She wore a tight, black miniskirt that fell inches from her waist, a black stretch tube top that only partially covered her breasts, and a short, black leather jacket decorated with silver zippers.

Six-inch, strappy, black stilettos held her feet, and a short, blond, pageboy wig covered her head. The large wording at the top of the poster read HUMAN TRAFFICKING.

Human trafficking? But that looks familiar.

I didn't understand. My eyes fixated on the picture as my fingers dragged across the girl's jacket. An uneasiness stirred inside. Her jacket looked like one I'd once owned.

I picked up one of the flyers that sat on the table next to the poster and turned to Sarah, my pastor's wife, who'd been browsing the tables with me. "I'm going to this workshop."

Later that evening, during chapel, I found my mind wandering. The room was alive with singing, praising, and the keynote speaker's message, but I couldn't focus. My mind kept rolling back to the image of the girl on the poster. Why did she look so familiar? Did I know her? My mind raced with questions and thoughts about the words "human trafficking."

That night, sleep eluded me. The next morning, as soon as breakfast was over, I quickly made my way to the conference room listed on the flyer. I found a seat in the back, my small attempt to remain incognito. Just as the speaker started, Sarah slid in beside me. We turned our attention to the podium up front.

"My name is Shari Neal Sanderson," the speaker began. "Thank you for coming. We will spend the morning learning about a little-discussed evil—human trafficking. There are more than twenty-one million people who have been forced into human or sex trafficking at any one time. It's a growing problem, even in the United States. It is going on right where you live. You may have even seen it and not known."

The speaker turned and clicked her mouse to start a video on the projection screen behind her. I watched intently, almost in slow motion, for several minutes. The girl in the film caught my attention.

Wait! That's me! That girl is me! At least the girl I had once been.

My heart beat fast and then faster, pounding in my ears. My head reeled and left me dizzy and nauseous. Something wasn't right. I wanted to run away, but I couldn't move.

Slowly my spirit began to lift from my body. Looking down at myself, visions from my past life flashed before me. One right after another. Bits and pieces, like the flash of a camera's light. Scenes of conversations with women I once knew played out. The stench of garbage on the streets I once walked swirled in my senses. My nostrils filled with the body odor and foul breath of men who'd paid for the unspeakable services I was forced to provide. The pimps who'd once controlled me, the drugs that had once quieted me—*pop, pop, pop*—hundreds of details, all of it at once. *Pop, pop, pop*—the images surged stronger and stronger. My breathing became more labored. I gasped for air.

Girl, you know this is pimping. Why are you playing with me?

The words shrieked into my ears. Heavy, musk cologne overpowered my senses.

Don't mess with me. I spent all this time and money to bring you here, and you do this?

His full hand tightened around my throat, and fear ran through my frozen body. The horror came back full force. The demonic face and voice of the man who had kidnapped me ran before my eyes. The humiliating sounds of verbal attacks, and the degradation of being raped over and over and over flooded my mind. Vicious slaps burned my face once again.

It was as if it were happening at that moment, there in the back of the conference room. The pain of feeling worthless, hopeless. The fear, anguish, and shame rushed through me.

I struggled to maintain a consciousness of my surroundings. There were a million questions I wanted—no, needed—to ask. Questions I'd never thought to ask.

A moment of clarity gave me the answer to the most important one.

I was trafficked.

It wasn't your fault. I brought you here for a reason.

The soft voice spoke clearly, but I knew I was the only one who heard it. Shivers shot down my back.

And then, I jolted back to reality. My breath caught, and I became aware of streams of tears that covered my face.

Sarah turned to me. My head fell onto her shoulder as I whispered my confession.

"I was that girl. I was trafficked."

"Oh, honey. Let's go outside." Sarah lifted me by my arms from the chair. Holding on to each other, we walked out of the chapel into the much-needed fresh air.

"I want to talk to Shari."

"Are you sure?" Sarah wiped a strand of hair from my tear-drenched cheek. "This might be too much for you."

"Yes. I need to tell her." My voice quivered. "Let's go back."

The film and talk ended within minutes after we sat back down. Sarah gave me a head nod. I eased to the front of the room, took a deep gulp of air, and extended my hand to the speaker.

"My name is Debra Woods. I think I was trafficked."

I sobbed uncontrollably. Shari took my hands and looked into my eyes. I saw compassion in her face. Sarah slipped up behind me and squeezed my shoulder. The dam of shame burst, and I easily told my story to this total stranger. The story I didn't want anyone to know but couldn't stop from telling. I felt safe with Shari and Sarah. And I was.

Later that evening, without revealing my identity, Shari shared my confession with the audience. Before the retreat was over, two more women approached her with their similar stories. I wasn't alone. From deep within, I felt compelled to run and scream to the whole world, *something bad is happening!* I wanted to run to my former friends and tell them, *you are being trafficked.* I wanted to shout to the police, the community leaders, even to the President of the United States, *the women on the streets are not there by choice. Young girls and women are being kidnapped and sold. You need to stop this! You need to stop this now!*

After a short session on Sunday morning, the conference leader gave us a challenge. "Has God spoken to your heart this weekend?" she asked. "For the next forty-five minutes, I encourage each of you to find a place of solitude to be alone with God." After a brief pause, she continued, "Spend time in prayer, meditation, and listen for what He has for you."

Following her prompt, I wandered into the woods, away from the others, and found a fallen tree to sit on. The beauty of nature surrounded me—the towering redwoods, fragrant wildflowers, the sounds of a rippling creek, and the singing of birds. I breathed in deeply, filling my lungs with the fresh air before letting it out slowly. I thought of the truths God had revealed to me about my past and my friends who were still out there on the streets. I lifted my hands and prayed, "God what can I do?"

Tears filled my eyes. Slowly, a strong and heavy presence came over me. The thickness in the air consumed every breath I took. It was palatable. Although my chest pounded, I no longer felt alone. "God? Is that you?"

My heart and soul burst with unexplained joy I didn't want to end. God spoke to me clearly. I knew what He wanted me to do.

I left the serenity of the woods with a mission. I carried with me a heavy burden to rescue my friends and others from the existence of hopelessness in which I once lived.

But I had no clue as to how.

CHAPTER ONE

When I held my beautiful baby daughter, Debra Carol Woods, for the first time, I couldn't take my eyes off her. Everything about her filled my heart with love—her dark eyes, the wisp of brown hair, the smell of her newness, her helplessness, her innocence. I held her close and whispered into her ear, "I'm your daddy. I will always love you. I will always watch out after you." Never could I have imagined how hard that would be.

- JR WOODS

July 25, 1979—My Birth Date

Mom had a secret—a full-blown heroin and cocaine addiction. She birthed three daughters, Christine, Lisa, and me—Debra. I was named after Mom and was often called Little Debbie. My sisters and I all have different fathers. Christine and Lisa were both abandoned by Mom by the time they were six months old and went to live with their fathers. Somehow Mom regained custody of Lisa after she met my dad. He had custody of his oldest child, my half-brother David.

To the outside world, we looked like one big happy family of five. We lived in the small country town of Easton, California, near Fresno. Daddy's parents lived down the street from us. Grandma watched us when Mom needed help. On one occasion, Mom dropped Lisa and me at Grandma's, telling her she was going to the store. Mom didn't come back. After a few days, Daddy called Lisa's father's family, and they came to take her. Six weeks later, Mom came to pick up her things and her baby.

"I'm taking Little Debbie."

"Over my dead body!" Daddy's voice and eyes told my mother he meant it. She packed up her things and left without me.

Of course, I learned all this later. I was six months old when it happened, the same age Christine and Lisa had been when Mom left them. She remained absent from my life until I was five.

My first memory is of living in a big, two-story, white farmhouse with my grandparents, Daddy, and my brother David. In the back of the property stood a big, red barn where countless childhood memories were made. Chasing chickens and playing with our many cats and dogs kept us busy.

Daddy was a truck driver. This paid enough to make sure we had the material things we needed. The truth is, we barely scraped by. Grandma and Grandpa provided us with stability, and we grew up surrounded by Dad's eight brothers, two sisters, their spouses, and countless cousins. My grandparents, along with other family members, heavily involved themselves with the local and strict Pentecostal congregation. The weathered, red-brick, country church held one large room for meetings and smaller ones along the side for Sunday School classes. Women and girls kept their hair long, usually piled high in a bun, their dress lengths to the ankles, and wore neither makeup nor jewelry. God and church were the focal points of our lives.

Worshiping with song and raised hands filled our spirits every time the doors opened. Men and women prayed loudly and spoke in words I didn't understand. I once witnessed a crippled man enter the church with his walker, barely able to push himself along. After the elders prayed over him, he walked out on his own, praising God. Another time, a younger lady had crushed her foot. After the elders prayed over her, she didn't need her crutches. A healing was always cause for more celebration.

It gave me comfort to hear Grandma pray. Sitting at the door of her bedroom, I often heard her cry out to the Almighty for someone in trouble who needed a touch from God. Sometimes it was for protection, sometimes for healing, or a multitude of other reasons. She praised God, singing songs and speaking those words I didn't understand as she raised her hands toward heaven. I knew Grandma had favor with God. Her prayers were answered more often than I can remember.

One day I experienced a miracle of my own. I'd been born with a chronic earache. My ears hurt constantly. Daddy usually took me to the doctor. The medicine helped, but two weeks later my ears would ache again. This went on for several years. One night I lay on my bed thrashing in pain.

"Daddy, my ears, my ears!"

I'm not sure why he didn't take me to the doctor that night, but it could have been that he didn't have the money or because of the late hour. But this night, the pain wouldn't go away. Taking a puff of his cigarette, he blew smoke into my ear, hoping it would help. Nothing changed.

"Let me do something." Grandma eased her hip onto my bed. Placing her hands to cover both of my ears, she prayed—silently at first, with her eyes closed. Then audibly, pressing her hands against the sides of my head.

"Father God heal my precious Debra of her pain. Take it away. Make her well."

She finished by speaking in those strange words I could not understand. After several minutes of crying out to God, she took her hands away. A rush of heat ran up the sides of my face and through my head, and then I felt it—*pop!*

To this day, my ears have never hurt again. God healed me completely.

I projected myself as a happy child to the outside world, but on the inside, I yearned to have a mother like the other kids. Sometimes, when Grandma cuddled me in her arms, I'd ask, "Why doesn't Mommy want me? Why doesn't she love me?"

Drawing me tighter, she'd whisper, "You're very pretty and so intelligent. I am so blessed that you are in my life. I love you so much. Your Mama is just ill. Let's pray for her."

Her words and comfort made me feel special, but a hole deep inside existed that even the love of my grandma couldn't fill. At some point, I started calling Grandma, "Mama," pretending that she was.

Playing with Piggy, one of the neighbor's pit bulls, was always an adventure. She followed me everywhere. We hiked around the expansive yard and into the trees, miles from home. Piggy and I were inseparable. I was never afraid with Piggy beside me. When she had a litter of puppies, I watched in amazement as she cuddled, nursed, and protected them. Her litter was her priority. The love Piggy had for her puppies awoke in me the need for my own mother. I sighed as I stroked her back. "You're a good mother, Piggy. I wish I had a mother like you."

Piggy's love did not stop with her puppies or her human favorites. Two weeks after Piggy had a new litter, another dog died in childbirth, leaving three surviving puppies orphaned. My uncle brought them to Piggy, hoping she would care for them. She sniffed, licked, and pulled each puppy close with her paw, adopting and nurturing them as if they were her own.

Several years later, my cousin brought home Squaw, another pit bull. Her gorgeous brown fur and the white spots on her face and feet complimented her stoutness. She displayed a gentle nature, and I immediately fell in love with her. Squaw and I became fast friends. When she became pregnant, my young heart leaped with excitement, hoping I could witness the birth of her litter.

"Take those puppies away from her, take them away!" my cousin yelled. Someone in the yard ran over and grabbed each one as they were being born.

But not before Squaw bit the head off one and ate another.

CHAPTER TWO

Grandma and Grandpa instilled into my life faith in God. They taught me that if I was ever in trouble, I could cry out to Him and He would help me. One story settled in the back of my childhood mind that gave me hope in times of crisis. Grandpa told it over and over, but I never tired of hearing it.

Grandpa loved to sit on the front porch in his big, brown, wooden rocker padded with his favorite weathered, red-checked cushion. Usually, in the late afternoon, he would read his Bible. Afterward, he would bow his head to pray. I knew Grandpa was praying for his family—me included. When he was through, he'd shout, "Do you want to hear a story?"

My brother David and I quickly stopped what we were doing and ran to sit at his feet and anxiously waited for him to begin.

"Tell us about the storm," David and I would say in unison.

Grandpa would get a faraway look in his eye. After a few minutes of collecting his thoughts, he'd start: "When my country called me to war, I enlisted in the Navy as a gunner on a ship. It was close to Christmas in 1945. One day, the skies began to grow dark. It was the middle of the day, but I couldn't see my hand in front of me. Rain began to fall, and soon it began to pelt down faster and harder and heavier, the likes of which I had never seen before or since. The wind blew sheets of rain sideways as the sea began to roll and roll and roll. The ship tossed and turned in the massive sea. I struggled to stand up straight and put one foot in front of the other. Waves kept crashing and reaching high, higher, and higher. I knew we would be tossed overboard at any minute. I didn't want to die."

"Were you scared Grandpa?" I'd look up at him, my eyes wide and my heart thumping.

He'd lower his head. "I prayed to God to help me and those men on that ship with me. I asked God to allow me to live through the night. I wanted to see your Grandma again." After pausing, he'd continue, "When I finished praying, I looked toward the bow. A woman, who looked identical to Grandma, smiled back at me. She wore a long, flowy white dress. Her blond hair blew in the breeze. Reaching out her hand, she tilted her head and smiled at me. I could not reach her, but I knew she was an angel. A peace that I cannot explain flooded over me. Everything was going to be all right."

One time, after telling the story, Grandpa sat quietly for a minute, then put his hand over his heart. "Many men were thrown overboard and lost their lives that night, but God sent an angel to save me and my buddies."

"Do I have an angel?"

"You'll never be alone." Grandpa patted my head. "We all have an angel watching over us."

"Your mother is here," Daddy announced.

I stood back, not wanting to get too close. She was beautiful, thin, with reddish-brown hair and big blue eyes. She smiled at me and talked gently for a few minutes before stretching her arms toward me. I slowly walked into her tight embrace, welcoming her hugs. My face disappeared into her flower-scented hair. Encircled with the love of my mother, I didn't want to let go. My five-year-old heart leaped for joy—*Mommy. I have a mommy.*

Dad kneeled to my eye level. "Would you like to spend some time with your mom? You need to get to know her."

Mom had just been released from prison for dealing drugs. My grandparents had moved to Sacramento and were no longer available to watch me. Two of my aunts talked Grandma and Grandpa into moving to be near them. Someone needed to watch me while Dad was at work now that his parents were no longer available. I couldn't have been happier with the new arrangement.

I had a mom, and we were going to spend time together. Daddy dropped me off with Mom each morning. She took care of me, including driving me to and from school. Soon I stayed with her through the week and Daddy on weekends. I had a mom, a real mom. It felt nice.

When I was six years old, I spent my first Christmas season with Mom and her new husband. She had warned me, "Stay out of the closet. Your Christmas presents are in there," but I couldn't contain my curiosity. While Mom was in the shower, I snuck into the closet. There was a large wrapped gift with my name on it. My heart beat fast. Before I could stop myself, I opened one end of the package. I let out an audible gasp when I caught sight of the Rainbow Bright doll I'd asked Santa for and desperately wanted. With Christmas only a few days away, I wouldn't have to wait long to call her mine.

I was dreaming of playing with my new doll when I heard, "What are you doing? I told you not to look in the closet. Just for that, you will not be getting presents from me this Christmas."

"I'm sorry! I'm sorry!" My eyes welled with tears. I could see the anger flare in Mom's eyes, but surely she wouldn't take my doll away.

On Christmas morning, when everyone opened their presents, there was no present for me from Mom. No Rainbow Bright doll. I couldn't believe it. I cried on and off most of the day. Why was my mother doing this to me?

I could see displeasure in Daddy's eyes when he realized she had not given me a gift. She had promised him she had bought me a Rainbow Bright doll.

A few days later, Mom approached me with a stern expression. "Do you think you can keep yourself out of the closet the next time I tell you not to look?"

"Yes."

She handed me the doll. Just the doll. No longer wrapped and no longer in its box.

"Thank you," I said, but my heart held no joy. I grabbed my doll, hugged her to my chest, and ran to my bedroom. It was the first gift I ever received from Mama.

Daddy let me go visit with my mom often, I think because she seemed to be doing well. I was young and don't remember much, but I started to notice something was wrong. She seemed to nod off all the time. I now realize it was drugs. Strange men came over during the day. Men who stared at me with a smirk on their faces, making my stomach churn. When Mom told me, "Go into your room and play," I obediently did what she said, wanting to get away. It always seemed I was alone in my room for a long time, usually falling asleep before she came to get me.

My time with Mom was short lived. She ended up going back to prison.

October 1989

I was ten years old when Dad applied for me to have an overnight prison visit with my mom. It took a year, but I was finally approved. I was the first child permitted a three-day, unsupervised visit at the California Correctional Women's Facility (CCWF) in Chowchilla, California.

"You're going to spend a few days with your mom," Daddy said. I squealed with delight when he told me I was going someplace special and would get to stay the whole weekend with her. Mom was delighted. The truth is, she reached out to me only when she was locked up, but I always wanted to see her anyway. She was no longer married, but she had plenty of "sugar daddies." She asked one to send $200, then sent the money and a shopping list to us to buy groceries and supplies for our visit. My feet bounced down the aisles at the store, shopping alongside my dad. I still think of those moments when we had fun choosing the items on the list Mom sent.

I could hardly contain my excitement during the thirty-minute car ride from our home near Fresno to the prison. I felt intimidated by the gray wire fences around the place I knew held my mom. But my anticipation overcame my fear. I took Daddy's hand and bravely walked into the visitors' center, holding my overnight bag while Daddy carried the bags of food. I stood in line as men and women in uniform checked and found my name on the list.

"Come with me," an officer beckoned, taking the groceries.

I said good-bye to Daddy and bravely allowed myself to be led away by a total stranger. Following the guard, I walked through a bank of wrought-iron gates into a cage called a sally port. One gate closed before another opened. Once inside the yard, the officer pointed to a row of connected dwellings enclosed with chain-link fences and a small, freshly mowed yard.

As I approached the prison apartment, Mom stood at the gate waiting for me, dressed in blue jeans and a pale blue t-shirt. When she saw me, her face lit up and she held out her arms. I ran to her. The officer handed her the sacks of groceries, and together we walked into the simple, two-bedroom respite with a small kitchen, living room, and tiny bathroom.

The space smelled of Grandma's cleaning supplies, as if it had just been prepared. Every room was painted stark white and the floors were white concrete, without even a scatter rug. One bedroom had a double bed and the second held twin beds and a table on which to lay a few things. There was an open closet, but no hangers. A few games stacked on the table in front of the couch promised some fun time with Mom, but there was no color or warmth to the place, except my mother's smile.

We filled the refrigerator with frozen meals, treats, and milk. Cereal and snacks covered the kitchen counter—enough for several days. Mom and I spent the first day getting to know one another again. It was nice to sit at the table, just her and me, as we ate our meals together, sharing laughter and conversation. Mom told me stories of women who were in prison with her, and I told her about my friends and my excellent grades in school.

She looked at me and smiled. "I'm proud of you, Debbie. Keep doing well in school. You are special, and you're going to do something great in life."

I knew deep inside I would. My mother believed I would.

Mom allowed me to sleep in the same bed with her, giving me a deeper sense of being loved. Late into the night, she told me bedtime stories, perhaps ones she'd heard as a child. We fell asleep safely in each other's arms.

When I left on Sunday night, I carried with me the memory of our special time together—Mommy and me. A time when everything seemed right with the world.

Things would be different when she came home... at least I hoped so. My mom loved me, and I loved her.

CHAPTER THREE

Soon after my grandparents moved to Sacramento, Daddy lost his job. He moved David and me there, hoping to find work. Aunt Audie, Daddy's sister, welcomed us into her small home, but since it was easier on her family, Daddy stayed with his brother, telling us, "It's just temporary until I get a job."

Days turned into weeks, and then into months. Still, Daddy had no job. He looked so unhappy, barely ever smiling. Looking back, I think this was his rock bottom.

Daddy started going to church with my aunts and found Jesus again. David and I went with him. We loved sitting in church beside our dad. He had always been a good dad, but things got even better after that. The tension in the house eased up and happiness returned. After Daddy eventually landed a job with a trucking company, we moved into an apartment of our own.

My oldest sister, Christine, whom I had never met, contacted Daddy and asked if she could meet me. Daddy said yes.

Christine was twenty years old and living out on her own.

When she arrived, Daddy led her into the living room where I sat.

"This is your sister Christine." Daddy stood next to a young woman with long, blond hair.

My sister? Before me stood the most beautiful woman I had ever seen. Just like Mom, Christine was tall and simply gorgeous. My ten-year-old mind admired Christine, falling in love with her instantly. I had a sister, and she looked so much like my mom—*our* Mom.

After our first meeting, Christine drove two hours every Friday, for several months, and took me back to San Francisco to spend the weekends with her. She introduced me to theme parks. We spent whole days riding rides, eating cotton candy, and laughing. Once, we walked around Fisherman's Wharf and down to Pier

39. We stopped at each shop then we watched seals play in the water. I loved to see the kites flying high above in the sky, and we stopped to watch performers on the street. Some days we visited parks or went to the movies, and other days we just hung out and truly enjoyed each other. During those times, I grew to love my sister even more and felt secure that she loved me.

Christine always told me, "You are beautiful, Debbie, and so smart. You're going to be someone important when you grow up."

I loved hearing the praise from my big sister. She saw only the good in me and was the encouragement I needed—a lifeline. Later, when my family moved back to Fresno, our friendship continued.

♦ ♦ ♦

While we were still living in Sacramento, Daddy moved us into a mobile home park behind our grandparent's house. They watched David and me while Daddy worked. We were easier to care for and less demanding of their time as we grew older.

One afternoon, when I was twelve years old, my cousins and I were playing outside. A scraggly looking man drove up in a long, black car. He was dark, with long stringy hair and an unkempt beard. He slowed his car to a stop.

"Hey, pretty girl, can you tell me where the baseball park is?"

The man scared me. The tone of his voice sent chills up and down my spine. I didn't answer him. Instead, I sprinted home, just like I'd been taught to do if a stranger tried to talk to me. A few days later, I saw that man again, driving down the street towards me. I dashed to tell Daddy. He and one of my uncles wasted no time in running out of the house. They rushed the man's car, pulled him out, and started to yell and punch him, causing blood to spurt from his nose. After that, he disappeared and was never seen in the neighborhood again.

That incident bothered me though. What did he want?

Shortly after Mom was released from prison, she picked me up at Daddy's house and took me to her motel room. While we were there, a man knocked on the door. She let him in and told me to go play outside. This became normal with her. Once, I woke up from a nap where I was sleeping on the floor next to Mom's bed. I heard noises above me. My mom was rolling her body around with some strange man. I didn't understand then, but now I know exactly what she was doing. As I grew older, those memories triggered a rumble in my stomach, making me want to throw up. My mother entertained men while my embarrassed heart tore apart inside.

Even so, I often waited by the phone for Mom to call, willing it to ring. It rarely did. When she eventually did call, she'd promise to come to see me. We would always agree on a specific time, but she'd never show up. More than once I sat on the curb crying for hours, rocking back and forth, before finally giving up—my spirit crushed.

Once, Mom contacted Daddy and asked him to take me to Fresno to spend a few days with her. Daddy dropped me off at of one of Mom's friend's, fully expecting she would come soon and get me. I enjoyed being there the first day, but one day led to another. The grownups smoked something strange and acted funny. After three days, Mom still hadn't come. I asked to call my Daddy.

"Daddy, please come and get me. I don't like it here. Mom hasn't come."

"What?" After taking a breath, he calmed his voice. "I'll be there as soon as I can."

I knew he would come. He always did.

When Daddy told his employer he needed to go and rescue his daughter, his boss warned, "You needn't come back if you leave." Daddy left anyway and lost his job in the process. He landed new work with a waste management company in Hanford, California. Dad's brother, Merle, who was a chief in the Navy at Lemoore Naval Air Base, lived in the area. Thankfully, he took us in.

1991—Twelve years old

Even though we moved, Daddy allowed me to attend a summer youth camp with my friends from Sacramento. I loved the outdoors, the woods, and cool nights on sleeping cots in cabins. Even better was the time I spent with other kids my age, swimming, making crafts, and sitting around outdoor fire pits talking about Jesus and telling stories. My time there embedded in me a deeper sense of faith that changed my young life.

In a strict Christian youth camp, where most kids came from sheltered homes, my worldly experience and God-given boldness were alluring to the other kids. I quickly became the talk of the camp. Everyone wanted to be around me. The campers voted me the most inspirational for the week. I'm not sure I was all that inspirational, but I loved all the attention.

On the last night, our leader gave an altar call to those of us who needed prayer or wanted to accept Jesus as our Savior. I stepped out of the group and walked forward, with tears streaming down my face, into the open arms of a female counselor. I cried to her about my absent mother and how lonely I felt.

I told her, "I want God with me always," and gave my life to Jesus.

My prayers went deep that night. Suddenly, a hot flash rushed through me, hotter than the heat the night my ears were healed. I began to speak in tongues, the language I'd heard Grandma speak, but that I couldn't understand. I still didn't comprehend, but I learned the Holy Spirit was speaking through me. It was exhilarating.

This is how Grandma must have felt when she prayed and spoke this way.

From that moment on, I knew God would always be by my side, even when I wandered.

♦ ♦ ♦

July 26, 1992—My Thirteenth Birthday

No one had ever given me a party.

On my thirteenth birthday, I rode out into the country with my uncles and cousins to watch drag races—an illegal activity, of course. My uncles loaded their racing cars on their trailers. The rest of the family followed them out to the place the races would be held. The men unloaded their cars and lined up on the deserted road. The sound of revving engines excited me. One of my uncles stood holding a checkered flag. With a swoop of a hand, the cars sped off, leaving the smell of car fumes behind.

We screamed and yelled as we watched the race. Someone called the cops, but we were alerted they were on their way. Immediately, the racing stopped, and all the cars and equipment were quickly packed up. We sped off to meet at everyone's favorite restaurant.

When Dad, David, and I arrived, a waitress led us to the back room. I stepped through the door and lost my breath when I heard, "Surprise!" The out of tune singing of *Happy Birthday* delighted and surprised me. Uncle Larry had decorated the room with pink and white balloons. A white frosted cake with pink trim and thirteen pink candles sat on the table in front of me. It had my name, Debra, written on it. It was the most beautifully decorated cake and room I had ever seen.

There were no presents to open, but that didn't bother me. I loved being the center of attention, a princess, even if just for the night. Still, I wished Mom could've been there.

CHAPTER FOUR

My friends and I were eager to go to the Red Ribbon Drug Rally sponsored by Fresno State University. I entered my poem in a contest just for the event. Surrounded by thousands of local students, representing almost every high school in the area, I heard, "The first-place winner is Debra Woods." Putting my hand up to my face, I heard a gasp escape through my lips.

"I won! I won!" I yelled. A rush of pure exhilaration spread through my body. My smile could not be contained as I made my way down the bleachers to receive my ribbon and certificate. My heart pounded with joy when I walked on stage. Happy tears filled my eyes as my poem was read.

100% Drug-Free by Debra Woods
Walking and thinking brought you into my thoughts.
Sometimes you were there but most times not.
You have only one excuse for not being by my side,
For not comforting me when I cried out from fright.
The reason it is, which cannot be excused,
Is the truth about drug abuse.
But you taught me something when you entered your new BART home.
It was then I realized it had been through everything I was shown.
That through everything I've seen my choice had to be
100% absolutely drug-free.

I vowed that day to never do drugs like my mother.

Lori was just the friend I thought I needed.

She had been abandoned by her mother too, which drew us together. She was different from the girls in my family and my church friends. She was a year older than me, more developed, stylish, sophisticated, and pretty—all the things I wasn't, but thought I wanted to be. She had freedoms I didn't have. Boys looked at her. I wanted what she had—lots of attention.

Lori projected the look of a hip teen, but befriended me, even with my long plain dresses, straight brown hair that reached my waist, and a face unadorned by makeup and scrubbed daily. We spent hours walking along the canal banks where we lived. Lori had delicious secrets she willingly shared with me. She talked about the "fun" things she did with boys. When she lost her virginity, she called me first thing the next morning to tell me every detail. Her stories fascinated me. It all sounded so exciting.

"I'm tired of the way I am, Lori, but I don't know how to look like you."

"I'll teach you," she told me.

And she did.

The next few days, we lived in Lori's bedroom while she taught me how to be cool. I tried on her clothes. I learned to put on makeup, perm my hair, and dress more modern. More seductive. Daddy gave me an allowance, and we spent a lot of time at the mall. Soon, I loved the way I looked. Church became less important. I found reasons not to go.

Lori trained me in the art of flirting and how to act cute with boys. A tremor shot down my entire body the night I experienced my first kiss.

I wanted more of this.

♦ ♦ ♦

1994—Fifteen years old

By fifteen, my anger was growing. I didn't care about anyone or anything, and I took my feelings out on everyone around me—family, teachers, kids at school... it didn't matter. My grades plummeted. I went from a straight-A student to flunking out. I ditched school and became even more belligerent and disrespectful, if that were possible.

One day, Daddy asked me to go with him to visit a friend. I agreed to go. While I sat on their couch watching television, the cutest boy I'd ever seen in my life walked into the house and my life.

I flashed on a big smile and raised my eyebrows at him, just like Lori taught me.

"Hi, I'm Martin. What's your name?"

"Debra," I gushed.

Martin plopped down beside me. My heart jumped. After that, I made sure I was with Daddy every time he went there to visit.

When our relationship progressed, Daddy warned Martin, "You'd better not hurt my girl."

"Daddy I didn't take anything," I pleaded.

Daddy's friend moved in with us, and then things in the house began to go missing—guns, money, and other items. I was the first person Daddy blamed. Angry that he didn't believe me, I snuck out of the house to meet Martin. It took several days for the police to find me and bring me home.

Daddy met me at the door. "Debbie, I'm sorry for accusing you of stealing from me. John confessed; he took the items."

He tried to hug me, but I brushed him away. Even though John had been arrested and booked into jail, it was too late. Daddy didn't trust me and accused me of stealing from him. I didn't want to let him forget it.

Something inside me changed from that incident. It gave me something to throw up in Daddy's face. My attitude went from bad to worse. I was going to do what I wanted to do, and nobody was going to stop me.

Eventually, my dad couldn't handle me anymore, so he allowed me to go live with my grandparents, who had moved back to the Fresno area.

And into the same neighborhood as Martin.

CHAPTER FIVE

Living at my grandparents gave me more opportunity to do what I wanted. Grandpa now had full-blown Alzheimer's. He didn't recognize me most of the time and always seemed confused. After Grandma went to bed, I'd sneak out of the house, waving good-bye to Grandpa as I left. He'd wave back and keep quiet, except the one time he asked Grandma, "Did that girl sneak out of the house again?" Fortunately, no one paid attention.

I ran to meet Martin almost every night. We'd sit together on a fence between my grandparents' house and his. At first, we'd spend about thirty minutes talking. But over the days and weeks, the time grew longer and longer. One morning, the paperboy met me as I walked back up to the house.

Grandma was up and stood outside waiting for me.

"Debra Carol, where have you been?"

"Nowhere. I'm tired and need to take a shower." I hurried past her into my bedroom. Picking up a few things, I stuffed them into my backpack and headed for the bathroom. After turning on the shower, I climbed out the window. I don't think anyone tried to find me or list me as missing. When I returned several days later, Daddy came right away.

"Sit down!" He took my arm and gently pushed me down on the couch. He sat down beside me and looked me in the eyes. "What is going on? What am I going to do with you? You need to stay away from that boy. I love you, baby, but you can't keep doing this." His body shook, and the tears that ran down his face scared me, but my anger and resentment remained strong. I wasn't about to listen to Daddy or anyone else for that matter.

My disrespect for teachers and my failing grades got me kicked out of high school. Around that time, my uncle and his wife, the parents of a two-year-old daughter, were in the middle of a divorce. It was arranged that I would move in with my aunt and go to continuation high school. While she worked nights as a waitress, it was my responsibility to watch her toddler. I did okay at school for two whole weeks. In the third week, I was called into the counselor's office for ditching and insulting a teacher. "We don't think our school is a good fit for you," the counselor said.

Home studies seemed to work well, except that I had to be in the apartment twenty-four hours a day. My niece needed to be watched during the day while my aunt slept, as well as when she worked at night. "You cannot have friends over while I'm gone, especially boys," my aunt warned me.

"I won't. Promise."

But as soon as she'd leave, Martin would knock on the door. On one of those nights, I lost my virginity. It wasn't planned. It just happened. It was quick, painful, and frankly embarrassing.

My aunt came home early from work one night to find us snuggling on the couch. Her face turned red as she pointed her finger at Martin. "What is he doing here?"

My aunt sent me home to Daddy.

I had sex with Martin only that one time, but that was all it took. One morning I woke up feeling sick. I'd missed my period and suspected I might be pregnant. A friend's mom worked for Planned Parenthood and kept several pregnancy tests at home. The first one I took came up positive.

This can't be.

I took a second test... Same thing.

No. This can't be!

I ended up taking five tests, each time hoping for a different result. But, by the end, I couldn't deny it. I was pregnant.

I decided it was best to get it over with, so I called Daddy right away. I blurted it out as soon as he picked up the phone. "Daddy, I'm pregnant."

Silence.

My body tensed, waiting for what felt like several long minutes for him to answer. "Are you going to spend the night at your friends?"

"Yes, I am, Daddy."

He hung up. A cloud of sadness overwhelmed me.

The next day, Daddy stared at me when I walked through the door. I could see tears in his eyes. He engulfed me with his arms and held me tight. After that day, Daddy was different, no longer the happy man I knew. The sparkle in his eye disappeared. The once talkative man grew quiet and barely had a word to say. My heart broke to see him that way, but I still knew I could count on my daddy.

Martin, my baby's father, was nineteen years old. I had no choice but to sign up for welfare and find a doctor on my own. Daddy and the rest of my family chose not to talk about my pregnancy. It was like it wasn't happening. No one acknowledged my bulging stomach until it was impossible to ignore. By then, I knew it was a boy, and with only a few months before my due date, it was time to prepare for his birth.

I lived with Daddy and even started to do better in school. Everything seemed fine between Martin and me, except for the rumors I heard about him hanging out with other girls. One night, he called. When I answered the phone, I heard his voice. It wasn't friendly.

"I don't want to see you again. I'm breaking up with you."

"But I'm carrying your baby."

"That's your problem, not mine. You're the one who got pregnant."

My lips quivered as my eyes filled with tears. "I thought you loved me. I thought you were my boyfriend."

"You're not my girlfriend."

"You said you loved me. I thought you were my boyfriend!" I repeated, screaming at the top of my lungs. I threw the phone receiver to Daddy, and fell to the floor, wailing. I thought he would get mad and tell Martin he had to keep seeing me, but Daddy calmly picked up the receiver.

"Martin?"

I heard Martin's response. "Yeah?"

"I warned you, and you didn't listen. You stay away from Debra. You do not have to worry about this child. As far as I'm concerned, this is not your baby. I will take care of him." Then Daddy hung up before Martin could say more.

"Daddy, why aren't you mad at him?" I blubbered, still sitting on the floor. "I can't believe you're not going to do anything. Daddy!"

"I told you to stay away from him. You are living the consequences of your choices. But you don't have anything to worry about. I will take care of you and your baby."

Deep sadness overcame me to know how much I'd disappointed Daddy, but he stepped in and kept his promise to make sure my baby and I had everything we needed. I felt safe.

Still, I thought if Martin saw his son, maybe he'd change his mind and want to be in his life. Daddy promised he'd call Martin when it came time for the baby to be born, but he tried to prepare me. "Don't expect him to show up, Debra. Don't set your heart on it."

The fact that I was due to give birth any day didn't stop me from spending the day at the car races, where my uncles had entered their car. I stood in the middle of the action, waiting breathlessly for the engines to roar. Then—*varoom*—the sound of twenty-five race cars shook the ground below my feet.

But that wasn't all that shook.

The pain grabbed me and took me to my knees. "Daddy, I think I'm going to have the baby." Daddy wasted no time. Once I was sitting securely in his truck, he drove over the speed limit to the hospital.

The doctor there checked me. "You're not quite ready to deliver. I'm sending you home for now."

Although I'd attended Lamaze classes with my friend, I wasn't prepared. I should have paid better attention in class. The labor pains came and went during the night, leaving me unable to sleep. Daddy called the doctor to tell him what was happening.

"It sounds as if Debra is getting too exhausted. We might want to induce labor. I'll meet you at the hospital."

Daddy called Martin and asked him if he wanted to go. He did, so we stopped and picked him up on the way. It felt good to have my baby's father with me. I hoped he would hold his son and want to be his fulltime dad.

Andrew was born on May 15, 1996, two months shy of my seventeenth birthday. When the nurse put my son in my arms, my heart stopped. I stared at him. He was just perfect—ten toes and ten fingers and plenty of black hair covering his tiny head. A lump of indescribable joy wedged in my throat. "You're so beautiful." It only took a few minutes alone with him for my heart to be filled with love.

When Martin walked into the room, I passed our son into the arms of his father. Martin stared at him in amazement. After a few minutes, Martin handed his son to my daddy. Then he grinned, nodded to me, and left. My heart sank, but there wasn't anything I could do to make him want us.

Cradling his grandson, my father focused entirely on Andrew. A big smile came over Daddy's face. After months of sadness, his joy instantly returned. "I'll take care of you, baby. Don't you worry," he whispered into Andrew's ear. And I knew he would.

Daddy held him for the next five hours, except when Andrew was hungry or needed to be changed. A bond formed between grandfather and grandson that day, one that would never be broken.

I didn't have sex again until my son was a year old.

I've always suspected that Martin was scared off by someone, who pointed out, by California law, I was underage and pregnant.

Grandma came to help with the baby, but Daddy took control. When I tried to get Andrew out of his bed in the morning, Dad would walk through the door and picked him up first. I loved being a mommy for a few months, but the newness soon faded.

I was ready to go back to my life of freedom. One day, Daddy walked into my bedroom. There was obviously something on his mind.

"Andrew needs a stable environment. If you can't give it to him, I will. You are not going to hurt him."

I eventually enrolled in a new high school. This time I earned straight As. One day, my teacher advised me that the school counselor wanted to see me. "Because of your poor grades your freshman year and the time you missed, there is no foreseeable way for you to graduate. You are aging out of the public school system and will need to finish your schooling in adult school."

I edged forward in the chair, confused. "What?"

I suddenly realized everything I would miss out on. I wouldn't get to go to the prom, high school football games, or enjoy high school life. All because of my life choices. There was no one else to blame.

I chose to work through my disappointment and enrolled in adult school. I took two math classes and passed everything with As. I took the high school GED and passed on the first try. It was time to move on.

CHAPTER SIX

Daddy married, and we moved into his new wife's home. This didn't sit well with me. I'd had Daddy all to myself most of my life and was unwilling to share him.

Daddy continued to worry aloud about the provocative way I dressed and the boys I seemed to attract. He tried his best to keep me out of trouble, but I grew increasingly hateful and harder to control. His rules were strict, made worse by my new stepmom.

My disrespectful behavior, talking back, disregarding requests to help around the house, having a sour attitude, were all part of a plan to get my way. I wanted to be with Mom, where I knew I would have more freedom. She didn't worry about me like Daddy did. Despite the fact that I was a mother myself, my survival depended on and was controlled by my Daddy.

There was one foreseeable way out, so I did what any rebellious teenager would do in my situation. I lied.

"Mom's doing really good and not drinking. I wanna spend more time with her," I told Daddy. Frustrated and tired of dealing with me and the friction I caused in the house, he chose to believe me and let me go live with Mom. There was just one catch.

"You need to figure out your future," Daddy told me. There was no way he would let Andrew go live with his reckless mother and grandmother. Andrew was one year old now, and I knew he was safe. And I was restless.

Within a few weeks, I voluntarily handed legal guardianship over to Daddy and ran to Mom. The call of freedom was just too powerful.

Mom had ideas, now that I was a young woman. She had lessons to teach me—how to hook a man, how to dress, how to wear makeup and glamorize my body to look even sexier. I wanted to attract boys, so I soaked it all up. Meanwhile, I was being prepared for my future. Mom was grooming me, but I was too naïve to realize it.

"He's cute," I told Mom about a guy she brought home.

"You think so?" Mom winked. "Go talk to him. Do what he wants."

I walked outside to meet him but felt uncomfortable when he suggested we go somewhere and have a little fun. He tried to grope me, which scared me. I pulled away. "No, I don't want to."

"Call your mom out here," he demanded, then yelled at her, "You're disgusting. Your daughter has no idea what's going on."

It was true. I had no real idea about what was going on. Maybe the truth was, I didn't *want* to know.

Mom continued to train me to feel and be beautiful, use my body, and talk to men. If I looked right, I could get my way every time. But I wasn't selling my body like Mom.

She often brought home "dirty old men" and younger ones too. I saw Mom doing drugs and getting paid for sleeping with her "friends." Her behavior didn't change because I happened to be in the house. Even though I loved my freedom, my resentment for my Mom grew and rested in a deep hole inside of me. Most of the time I put on a good face, but alone with my thoughts, I seethed.

How could she do what she did to me? Why didn't she want me? How come she wasn't around when I was growing up? Why did she leave me by myself, playing outside of her motel room?

I knew what she'd done. I hated my mother for her life of drugs and men. I was sickened by what she did, but I was powerless to let go of the freedom that I had with her. Powerless over the want to be desired. But I kept telling myself I would never grow up to be like her.

Never.

I somehow managed to get my own apartment, which gave me even more of the freedom I thought I needed. My friends took advantage of my frequent invitations to get together and smoke weed. Mom often came over to party too. She wanted to be my friend but not my mom. My eyes were opened wide. I began to really see Mom for what she was. She disgusted me, and my anger continued to fester.

But my disgust couldn't stop what or who I was becoming. Nor did it occur to me that I *was* just like her, abandoning my child the same way she had done to me. Why would a mother do that? Why would I do that? I didn't have the answers.

I looked up and stared into a set of large green eyes. The contagious smile that spread over his face matched the sparkle in my eyes.

"Nelson?"

"That's me."

A light-skinned Puerto Rican man in his early thirties stood before me—all six foot four inches and 260 pounds of him. "Well, come in, Nelson." I motioned him in. My friend, Dizzy, had called and invited him to come over and meet me.

Nelson walked in the door and stayed. We spent the night getting to know one another. He had plenty of money, drove a nice car, and wore expensive jewelry. He took an instant liking to me. I soon didn't want for anything. He even bought me a new car. Nelson became my provider and my protection—may be too much of a good thing.

Nelson made his living as a drug dealer and sold illegal guns. While he had a drug habit, he didn't want me to. Life was good for five months, until one night I answered a phone call. "Hey, baby. I got arrested. I'm here in a holding cell."

"What happened?"

"The police found guns in my car." He sat in the county jail only a couple of days, then was released until his trial.

♦ ♦ ♦

Nelson knew he was on his way to prison, and I knew I had to find a job. An ad for a dancer piqued my interest.

This is perfect. It'll be fun.

The darkness of the nightclub, I'd learn, held deep secrets of the many who frequented it. The years of wild parties had left many a broken heart. The man who greeted me eyed me in a way that made me uncomfortable—dirty. But I would have to get used to that. The dance floor was staged several feet up from the guest area with a platform connected to the oval bar. Dancers could start on stage and continue their act along the top of the bar.

"Let's see what you can do." The owner slid into a chair and motioned to the man behind the bar. "Put some music on."

All I learned from Mom would come in handy here. Flirt, act naughty, and look them in the eye. That's how you get what you want.

What I wanted was plenty of tips to take care of myself and have a little fun.

The music started slowly. In my jeans, t-shirt, sandals, and sweater, I began to sway. I tilted my head back and forth a little as the music played. *I have got to land this job. Let go, Debbie.*

When the music came to a stop, I picked up my clothes and looked out into the audience. I could see several men—employees—who were whistling, clapping, and yelling, "Bring it on!"

"You want to start tonight?"

"Sure." *God, what have I done?*

"Go to Lucy's in the old town district. Have them help you pick out something to wear and bill me. Here's my card. Come back at nine, and we'll put you on. If the audience likes you, you have yourself a job."

My talent for keeping the men entertained generated quite an abundance of tips to supplement my income. Work was necessary, so I figured I might as well make as much as I could. I was a dancer—not like Mom. I *danced* for a living. That's what I kept telling myself.

But I took the drugs to bury my guilt.

CHAPTER SEVEN

Nelson wasn't keen on the idea of me dancing, but he didn't stop me. While he was out on bail, he continued to act as my protector and bodyguard, whether I wanted him to or not. I allowed him to be my boyfriend until I found out he had another relationship on the side with an older, rich woman. Nelson apparently had a thing about older and wealthy.

I tried to leave Nelson but found out it wouldn't be easy. When I told him our relationship was over, he seemed stunned. Without saying a word, he left but came back later wanting to talk. I allowed him back into my apartment.

Tears welled in Nelson's eyes when he asked, "It took two of us to decide to be together, correct?

"Correct." I pressed my hands on my hips.

"You may have decided not to be with me, but I have not decided not to be with you, girl."

It was a strange conversation, and while his emotional plea did nothing to move me, it did make me uncomfortable. "Well, you may have decided to be with me, but I have decided *not* to be with you. Right? Good-bye, Nelson."

Nelson left dejected, but he didn't give up. He continued to call and come over. Any effort to try and ignore or dissuade him didn't seem to matter. I just wanted to be rid of this relationship.

A few weeks later, my friend, Teri, brought two guys over—a date for her and one for me. Ted had been paired with me. He was short and small, very tiny compared to Nelson. The four of us were sitting and talking when the phone rang. It was Nelson.

"What are you doing?"

"Just hanging out," I responded, cocky.

"That guy you're with doesn't know who he's messing with."

"How do you know?"

Nelson quickly hung up without answering. He called back a few minutes later.

"What do you want, Nelson?"

"Tell him I'll be there soon."

"Tell who?"

"You know." *Click.* The phone went silent.

"That was Nelson again." I frowned, holding the receiver and looking at it. "He knows there are guys here, and he's upset."

"That guy ain't no problem for me," Ted scoffed.

Teri's date nodded. "We can handle him."

"This guy is big, guys. Real big," I warned.

Clearly worried, Ted fidgeted with his hands. But they both stayed. And nothing happened.

After an hour, Ted laughed. "He's all talk."

"I think we're going to get out of here," my friend said. Her date agreed. That left me alone with Ted. He glanced around the apartment. "Where is the bathroom?"

"Through my bedroom."

While he was in the bathroom, the phone rang.

Teri's breathless voice came over the receiver. "Nelson jumped over the fence and is on the way up to the apartment."

I quickly turned the bolt just in time, but Nelson had a key and used it.

"Where is he? Where is he?" Nelson yelled.

Ted heard the commotion and tried to hide behind the bathroom door. Nelson burst in, reaching for his gun. I followed to see Ted quickly jump from the bathroom window with his pants down, running away.

Nelson pointed out the window. "Good, he's gone. Running like a rabbit."

I narrowed my eyes. "Who do you think you are?"

Nelson walked into the living room and began to cry. "Why are you doing this to me? I love you."

"You're sleeping with other women. I don't want to be with you." The thought ran through my mind that this guy might be certifiably crazy. I knew people feared Nelson. I liked walking down the street with him for this very reason. No one was going to mess with me when he was around. But I really hadn't bothered to learn or admit how dangerous Nelson could be. With Nelson staking a claim on me, it kept other men away. Even so, I refused to go back to him, but he still came around and was in and out of my life.

Dancing supported me, but it wasn't enough. I decided selling drugs might be the perfect solution. I moved to a new apartment right into the midst of drug trafficking.

The people in my new neighborhood weren't exactly the type you take home to meet most mothers, but they were perfect for mine.

Mom moved in with me. I met a new guy, Dutch. He was as big, strong, and as mean looking as Nelson. I wasn't worried. Dutch could take care of himself.

I gave up dancing.

One morning, I heard the rumble of a familiar engine outside. I looked out the window and caught Nelson's large black vehicle coming down the street.

"Shhh" I whispered to Dutch.

Startled by the knock on the security door at the bottom of my second-floor apartment, fear crept into my voice. "Be quiet. We can't let Nelson know we're here."

The rapid banging became louder with the sound of urgency. We stayed silent, holding our breath. When Nelson finally left, I sighed with relief.

A few minutes later, I heard Nelson's vehicle enter from the other side of the apartments. The security gate clanked, alerting me he was back. We were in trouble.

We didn't call the cops because we had drugs in our possession. I knew I had to face up to Nelson or he would stalk me until he found me. Wrapping a towel around my head as if I had just stepped out of the shower, I opened my door and started down the stairs.

Nelson looked up at me, sadness in his eyes, teeth clenched. "Debbie, I love you with all of my heart, but if you don't open this gate, I'm going to take you and your friend out."

I knew Nelson wasn't playing around. However, my concern was for Nelson. I believed he had finally met his match.

The apartment door opened, and Dutch stepped outside. He started to open his mouth to say something, but before he could, his face met Nelson's fist. Taking Dutch in a headlock with his left arm, Nelson punched him over and over with his right fist. Dutch seemed helpless to defend himself.

"Stop! Stop!" I cried.

I tried to get Nelson away from Dutch. Nelson shoved me away and reached for Dutch's head, twisting his neck. Dutch did his best to defend himself, but Nelson was clearly too strong. Was he going to break his neck? My eyes and mind went numb in disbelief.

"Why don't you listen?" Nelson asked Dutch. "This is my wife," Nelson repeated these words over and over several times.

I'm not his wife. What is he talking about?

Dutch had called a taxi before he came out of the apartment. When the cab pulled up, Nelson allowed him to stumble toward the cab, holding his head, blood dripping through his hands.

"Never come back here again," Nelson yelled, pushing Dutch into the back seat. He slammed the door shut and turned to me. "Let's go to breakfast."

I didn't dare say no, but I couldn't believe what had just happened. "Let me get dressed," I managed to squeak out.

What I'd just witnessed left me nervous—very nervous. I turned on the hair dryer to make Nelson think I was getting ready, giving me time to think.

On the way to the restaurant Nelson informed me, "I'm going to stop at the hardware store and get a key made." I decided not to argue with him. Nelson bought me a red rose before we left the store. He drove to breakfast, but I wasn't sure I could eat.

"I love you, Debbie. I'm sorry for the way you feel about me," Nelson cried when we were seated in a booth.

I sat across from him speechless.

After Dutch, Nelson tried even harder to control my life, always watching me. I sold drugs. I used a little, at least until Nelson started to threaten those who sold to me. I soon lost my inventory and my connections.

Eight months after he was arrested, Nelson went to trial on a complex gun charge and was found guilty. The judge sentenced Nelson to two years in prison. He wasn't watching me anymore. I could breathe easier.

I got evicted. Through my mother, I met Darnell and Darryl. They were a pimp team, though I didn't realize it at the time. I thought they were just friends. Darnell was blind and needed someone to help him with day to day activities and chauffeur him. He allowed me to move into his house. He had a son, Charlie, who would soon graduate from high school and played football. Charlie liked me and didn't cause me any trouble.

For four months, I helped Darnell with personal care, house cleaning, and cooking. One of my duties was to drive Darnell where he wanted to go, usually out to the area where pimps and drug dealers hung out. We were there to collect money from those who worked for him on the streets.

One night I witnessed how vicious Darnell could be. He was upset with one of the women he visited every night, but I didn't know why.

"Come to the window," he coaxed one of his girls.

For some reason, she seemed reluctant. She finally got close enough to the car, and he yanked her by the hair and pulled her through the window. Screaming obscenities at her, he shoved his fist into her face repeatedly until blood began to ooze from her mouth. When he finally let her go, he took all her money and left her with nothing. My mind couldn't take in what had just happened.

"Drive on," he ordered.

Stunned, I did as he said.

♦ ♦ ♦

Daddy and the rest of my family were fed up with my self-centered and rebellious behavior. My mother's addictions to alcohol, drugs, and men who paid for her favors were not my addictions. At least that's what I told myself. Yes, I undressed every night in front of men, but that was dancing, nothing more. And I could stop taking drugs anytime. I was sure of it.

"You're no good. You're just like your mom. You'll never amount to anything." I was told these things by my family more often than I could count.

"I will never be like Mom. She makes me sick. I will take care of myself," I told them. I just couldn't take care of my son right then.

Deep inside, where no one else could see, the girl who looked back at me in the mirror began to repulse me. Was she more like her mother than she wanted to admit? She had missed her high school years. She had a child who she couldn't care for and no husband. The girl in the mirror had grown angry, bitter, and resentful. The girl in the mirror was totally ashamed of who she had become. The pain I saw in the mirror reflected what had been lost.

The girl in the mirror was easy prey.

CHAPTER EIGHT

February 1999

How could I have been so stupid? Did some part of me know?

It's difficult to detail this part of my story, because of all the self-imposed blame, shame, and guilt. I must tell it, though, to free myself and to free others.

In the cold February air, I noticed a good-looking guy in the hotel parking lot across the street from where I stood. I motioned to my friend, Brandy. "Look at that fine thing."

"You don't want to go there. Let's get out of here."

Once we got into the safety of her car, I asked her, "Why? What's his name?" I swore I had just seen the most gorgeous man I'd ever laid eyes on. Why was she so afraid?

"His name is Thomas. Trust me, you don't want to get mixed up with him. He's bad news. Let's go." Her nervousness concerned me. She clearly didn't want him to see her, but he looked harmless to me. He just looked good.

A few days later, I saw Thomas again. My eyes met his flirtatiously like my mother taught me. He folded his arms, turned toward me, and gave me a big smile. "Come here, girl," Thomas beckoned. "I noticed you girl the other day. You're Darnell's friend, huh?

"I just work for him. You know, drive him around and help him."

Watcha doing tonight?"

"Why?"

"I have this room rented for the weekend." He gave me a sideways glance that sent a thrill up my spine. "Why don't you come party with me?"

Thomas was a little taller than me, around five foot ten. He wore black pants, a black and white jacket, and a black shirt. His shoes and hat complemented his clothes and dark skin, making him even more appealing. I couldn't believe this man was talking to me.

I ignored my friend's warnings. I couldn't help myself. "Sure. I'll be there in a few minutes."

Somewhere in the back of my brain, an alarm went off. Something wasn't right here. Something about the way he looked. The word "evil" popped into my mind, but I quickly dismissed it. I could handle myself, so no need to worry. I was a big girl.

That night, we hung out together, smoked weed, and partied. My time with Thomas felt electric. Thomas had recently been released from prison for drug dealing, but he assured me he was getting his life on track and wouldn't be going back.

The next few weeks, Thomas stayed in my life, and I decided to start dancing again. Thomas went to the club every night to watch me dance. His eyes lit up when I performed. He wouldn't tell me what he did for a living, but whatever it was, it made him a lot of money. Thomas took me to a Rhythm and Blues concert where he introduced me to the stars of the show. I heard them on the radio every day and was impressed that Thomas not only knew these guys but seemed to be close friends with them.

Thomas continued to show enormous interest in me, which I ate up. I felt secure enough to spend hours telling him about my problems. He listened and allowed me to believe that his heart was filled with sympathy toward me.

Other things interested him too. I shared my dreams. "I want to go back to school, get a better job, and make a good life for my son. One day, I hope to make something of myself, maybe get a college education."

"Those are big dreams." He smiled.

A few days later, Thomas treated me to breakfast. That's when he hit me with a proposal. "You know I'm no longer about selling or doing hard drugs, but I do know a way you can make some fast money." He winked and took a sip of coffee. "Twenty-five thousand. Easy money."

"Really? How?" This couldn't be for real.

He looked me in the eyes. "You're beautiful. Smart too." He showered me with lots of flattery. I melted inside, feeling more loved and sexier every time he complimented me. I began to believe I was the most gorgeous woman in the world.

"I can take you to Los Angeles." Thomas leaned over the table. "There's a need for high- class escorts. All you have to do is have dinner and entertain wealthy men. That's it."

"That's all? You would do that for me?"

He sat back confidently. "That's it. I just want to help make you happy."

"You think I can?"

"You're so gorgeous, it will be easy."

Thomas made me feel beautiful. He had a way of making me feel valuable that no one else had before. My eyes sparkled as he continued to tell me what I wanted to hear. "When you get back, you'll have the money you need to set yourself up in a new apartment and start school. You'll be able to take care of your son. Everything will be great."

Somewhere deep inside, I knew I shouldn't trust this man. But I ignored my gut. Maybe he was telling the truth. I really could use the money. Twenty-five thousand was more money than I had ever seen. I could go to Los Angeles for a few weeks, make a lot of money, have a good time, and come home. That would be it.

"Sounds good."

CHAPTER NINE

March 1999

Thomas picked me up for the drive from Fresno to Los Angeles. Before we rolled away from the curb, he gave me a serious look. "I want to make one thing clear. You're not my girlfriend. We just have a few laughs and sex. That's all."

"Then why are you doing this for me?" Why was he saying I wasn't his girlfriend? I thought he loved me.

"Because I like making gorgeous women happy. Making you happy will make me happy."

An uneasiness stirred in the pit of my stomach, but soon we were speeding down the freeway, heading south to Los Angeles. Thomas mostly kept quiet. Rap music came from the radio, breaking the awkward silence. Thomas seemed to be somewhere else, but he intermittingly said phrases like: "This is going to be great. You're so beautiful, every man is going to want to take you to dinner. You're going to live the high life." His words lifted my spirits with hope and promise.

"I should go into a new line of work—protecting women. There's a lot of tax-free money to be made. I can take care of my girls, and they will take care of me." Looking straight ahead, Thomas continued. "I don't like going to prison. Drug dealers go to prison. Pimps don't. The girls are the ones on the streets. The cops arrest them. It's easy money for me."

Excitement tinged with a bit of nervousness filled my stomach. Why was he talking like this?

In the late afternoon, Thomas stopped for gas. We were about half-way to Los Angeles. When I stepped out of the car to find the restroom, I heard a voice.

Something bad is going to happen, and it will affect the rest of your life.

Who was that? I didn't see anyone. An overwhelming sense of dread wrapped around my mind. My hands shook. Maybe I shouldn't get back into the car.

I swallowed the warning, shoving it back into my gut. I was being silly. Thomas was good to me. I might not be his girlfriend, but I knew he loved me. Why would he change?

But why is he talking about pimping? He's not a pimp. Still, I need this money. I can handle this. I'm a big girl.

I kept my thoughts to myself and got back into the car.

Thomas continued to drive toward Los Angeles, and I continued to wonder if I had made a mistake. It was evening when we arrived at a nice hotel in the heart of Hollywood. The lobby looked fresh and clean. Everything seemed normal. Families and business people came and went. I felt a bit more at ease.

We stepped on the elevator to go up to the third floor and found our room quickly. When the card key slid into the holder, it opened into a newly freshened, white and beige room with two beds. One for me and one for Thomas, I guessed.

I was right. It's okay.

After freshening up a bit, I walked out of the nearly all-white bathroom to see condoms scattered on my bed—at least two dozen of them. A wave of nausea took me back. I had just walked into something, and it wasn't good.

"What are those for?" I pointed at the pile of condoms on the bed.

"You know what they're for."

"I don't do that. I'm a dancer, not a prostitute. I came here to escort men, not to have sex with them."

"Girl, this is pimping. I thought you knew," he yelled. "Why are you playing with me?"

The words shrieked into my ears. The smell of his heavy musk cologne filled my senses as he raised his hand, threatening to slap me.

"No, no, no. Wait a minute. I don't do this," I stammered.

"Don't mess with me. I spent all this time and money to bring you here, and you do this?" The grip of his full hand tightened around my throat and fear rippled down my back.

"You're mine. I own you. And you're gonna make me lots of money."

Thomas's fist collided with my face, causing severe pain to shoot through my jaw. Had he broken something? He pushed me onto the bed. I lay unable to move for a several minutes.

Thomas had tricked me, and I didn't know how I would get out. Nothing in my Christian upbringing or my days of rebellion had equipped me for this. My mother didn't prepare me for this. How did I get here? *Oh, God, help me.*

"I want to go home."

"Well, if you want to go home, you'll have to get us there. This is no game. What did you think you were gonna do?" He was angry, and nothing I could do would change his mind.

Grabbing my shoulder, Thomas pushed me to the floor, raised his hand, and hit me about the head. He picked me up, threw me on the bed, and violently raped me.

Afterward, I crawled under the bedcovers, stunned and confused. "Why?" I cried out to him.

"You need to shut up." He smirked. "Go to sleep. I have appointments set up for you tomorrow. I need you to be fresh."

I curled up in a fetal position, silently sobbing. Even if I could get to a phone, there was no one to call. Daddy had told me he'd had enough. I shamed and embarrassed him for the last time. Mom didn't care. Just me now, and I was alone—so alone.

I'm here, I won't forsake you.

When I awoke the next morning, Thomas wasn't in the room. He had gone downstairs for breakfast. He came back with a tray of food for me. "Eat girl," he demanded. "Then get into the shower. We have work to do today." He acted as if nothing had happened.

After showering, I stepped out of the bathroom and eyed the clothes laid out on the bed—a pair of tight black pants and a red sweater. "Put these on. When you bring in some money, I'll buy you some nicer clothes." I stood, frozen. He stared at me for a moment and then his voice became stern. "*Get dressed.*"

Once I was fully clothed, Thomas sat on the other bed and told me the rules. "This is what I'm telling you to do. You better listen. These rules are to protect you and my investment."

"Your *investment*?"

"Don't play with me." He sneered, grabbing my arm. "Always wear protection. I'll make sure you have a supply of condoms. Don't look at other pimps. You're my property."

His property? His *property*? Why was he talking like this?

He continued. "Always collect money upfront. You don't want them getting away without paying." His jaw tightened. "Avoid the police. They'll arrest you and put you in jail. And, whatever you do, don't tell them about me. They won't believe you anyway. Do you understand?"

"Yes." The answer came out in a raspy whisper.

"Be careful who you get in the car with. Don't be fooled by an undercover cop or another pimp trying to recruit you. Make sure the doors stay unlocked. You might need to escape."

I sat there, embarrassed by the situation I found myself in. Thomas sounded nervous as he spoke but didn't hold back. "Don't fight back. If he threatens you and doesn't give you money, let him have what he wants and get out."

I gulped and nodded.

He pointed his finger at my nose. "No drugs. Just the weed I give you."

How was I going to get myself out of this? I was living in a nightmare. *God, help me.*

"If you break any of these rules, there will be a price to pay." He stood over me. "I'll give you everything you need. Food, clothes, everything. You won't need money. I'll take care of it for you." Thomas paused and glared into my eyes. "You got that?"

In a brief attempt of strength, I sputtered. "You said I would make money as an escort."

"Shut up! Let's go."

Trepidation sat in the pit of my stomach. *I can't do this. I can't. I want to go home.*

But I wasn't going home anytime soon.

CHAPTER TEN

Still reeling from the night before, my heart raced as Thomas clutched my arm and walked me out through the back door of the hotel to my "appointment." On the short drive, I sat quietly, hoping it wasn't real. A silent prayer went up to heaven.

God, only You can deliver me.

Thomas pulled up to a nice apartment complex in a high-end neighborhood. "Get out of the car and stay with me."

The guy who answered the door was tall, heavy, and unkempt. He looked like he'd been up all night.

"Here she is." Thomas pointed to me with a nod.

Handing Thomas cash, the man grabbed my hand. "Get inside." I did as he said, the feeling of dread heavy around me.

"I'll wait outside until you're through." Thomas snickered.

The man closed the door and motioned me to his bedroom. Frightened, I stood and stared at him defiantly. Shoving me lightly, he forced me to go with him. He pulled my body down on his unmade bed and groped me. His garlic breath and sweaty body odor nauseated me. Unwilling to participate, I laid there, unresponsive, sending my thoughts somewhere else. This isn't happening. Make it go away.

After he raped me, he took me outside and yelled at Thomas. "This girl's no good. She acted like a mummy. I want my money back." He raised his fist in Thomas's face. "You gotta do better than this if you want my business. Or anyone else's, for that matter."

Thomas handed the money back, but his tight frown told me I was in trouble. We drove back to the hotel in dead silence. Opening the door to our room, Thomas tilted his head, motioning me to go in first. He pushed my shoulder, making me fall into the room. I managed to get up, but when Thomas's fist bashed my back, I went to the floor.

He hit me with a series of punches, carefully avoiding my face this time. Doubled over in pain, I cried out. "Help me!"

Did anyone hear?

"Shut up! Shut up!" He kept hitting me. He lifted me up, but quickly pushed his foot to my back, forcing me back onto the bed. "You're no good. Nobody wants you. You're just a ho like your mama. But you're gonna be mine." His tone became louder and angrier. "You gotta do better. If you know what's good for you, you'll do as I say."

I lay there, shaking.

"I'm getting something to eat." He glared at me. "When I get back, you better have yourself together." He pointed his finger in my face. "I'm watching you."

I picked myself up and slowly walked to the bathroom. Stepping into the shower, I slid down into the tub as the water ran over my trembling body. Pulling my knees up to my chin, I rocked back and forth, crying out in my soul. What am I going to do?

Thomas allowed me to sleep through the afternoon. Even though my body was covered in bruises and in intense pain, he had another appointment for me that night. "You better give this man what he wants and act like you like it."

I'd have to get through this. I'd have to find a way to just get it over with.

Afterward, when he was satisfied the client was happy, Thomas grunted his approval. "Good job."

The next morning, Thomas drove to a street in a busy area. "Get out," he said, then peered into my face and warned, "I'll be watching you." He gave me twenty condoms and told me to use them all before coming back.

What do I do now? How would I know what Thomas wanted? Would he kill me if I got it wrong? What if I couldn't get a man to stop? What if the man I picked up killed me? What if?

I walked the street, peered into the windows of the cars that drove by and flagged down men who might be interested in what Thomas had to offer. It proved to be easier than I thought. There were so many men; men from every social class—old men, young men, large men, small men, rich men, working-class men, white men, Mexican men, Middle Eastern men, Asian men. Some were handsome, and some were ugly. Some smelled good, and some didn't. Some wore wedding rings. I'd have a "date" with one and there always seemed to be someone else waiting and willing to pay for my favors. My face revealed my true feelings, but I did what I was ordered to do—made my customers happy. When my quota was met, Thomas brought me in and offered me a little weed to smoke. It gave me some rest and helped ease my pain; physical, mental, and emotional. I wasn't allowed to use drugs, except for the little Thomas gave me.

I was a prisoner living in the middle of a nightmare, which pushed me into a deep depression. Disgusting, nasty old men picked me up. I had sex with them and took their money. The acts left me feeling dirty and physically ill as I struggled daily with the pungent smell of testosterone, sweat, and body odor. Many times, I found a bathroom after a "date" and vomited out the taste of the revolting mess. I just wanted to get it over with. I wanted my nightmare to go away, but no matter how many men I was with, there would be another, and another, and another. Usually twenty to thirty a day.

"How much?" the good-looking man with the great smile asked.

"Friday night special for you." I returned his smile. "Two hundred."

"Get in."

Sliding in beside him, I made eye contact and smiled a bit more. He hesitated before pulling away from the curb. Glancing in my side mirror, I caught the sight of two men getting out of the car behind me. My throat tightened. They were rushing up to the car. One pulled the door open and yelled, "Get out!"

Was I being kidnapped? Arrested? My body tightened.

"You are under arrest for soliciting sex," one officer said. They looked at me with revulsion, as if I was sub-human.

I'm not here by choice. Someone is making me do it. Someone is holding me against my will. I wanted to scream, but I was too afraid to tell them. They wouldn't believe me anyway. Thomas had told me so. I gave them an address that had been prearranged—my mother's. They ran my fingerprints and released me that night. It was my first arrest, but it wouldn't be my last.

"Stay off the streets or risk being arrested again," the officer warned.

It terrified me that I might be caught. Up to that point, I had never been in jail. Thomas reminded me to avoid the police, but it was impossible. I had been on the streets two weeks when Thomas announced, "We're going back to Fresno."

"Back to Fresno?"

"Yeah. I gotta check in with my parole officer, so we'll hang out there for a while. But don't get excited. You're still working for me." He laughed.

I laughed too, but my heart held hope. Would this be a chance for me to get away? I knew I couldn't call Daddy, but maybe there was someone I could call.

Once we were back in Fresno, Thomas got a hotel in a part of town that would make it easy to keep an eye on me. That night, he put me on the streets.

CHAPTER ELEVEN

There were many times I walked alone on the street, even on a cold night, dressed in boots, shorts, and a sheer top. Thomas sat in his car, drank his hot coffee, and kept his eyes on me. If I felt tired, I often waved at him and begged him to let me stop for the night. He'd smirk and say, "You're gonna stay out here until you meet your quota."

Sometimes that would be till three or four in the morning. And it started all over the next day.

Thomas moved me from city to city. We spent quite a bit of time in Los Angeles, where there was lots of money to be made. Since Thomas was still on parole, he had to check in with his parole officer every month in Fresno. We traveled to Stockton and the Bay area, always moving around. Every place we went, he expected me to work.

During a stay in Fresno, four months after being lured to Los Angeles, Thomas announced, "Get dressed. I'm taking you to get a tattoo. One to show that you're my property."

Property? I winced but knew better than to argue.

He drove me to a friend of his who gave tattoos out of his home—a self-trained tattoo artist. Tattoos like the ones I'd seen on friends who'd spent time in prison. Seeing the outside of the house, I hesitated. It looked unsafe. A fence surrounded a bed of dry, yellowed grass. Boxes and old papers were strewn around the yard. On the porch sat an old brown couch with several other chairs scattered in disarray. Heavily tattooed men sat outside in the middle of the afternoon and stared into space.

"How ya doin', Thomas?" a man asked, as he stepped out of our way.

Thomas nodded, held my arm, and nudged me inside.

The front room looked as trashy as the outside of the house. Dirty white foam poked out through two old brown leather couches. A table covered with cigarette butts, remnants of marijuana, and empty beer bottles sat in the middle of the room in front of the giant television screen wedged in the corner. The musty aroma of drugs, sweat, and liquor filled the room. A small space to the left held the makeshift tattoo parlor.

A big burly man sporting a full beard and long dreadlocks motioned us in. "Wait here."

Tears threatened to spill as I waited. *I deserve this. I won't cry.*

"Pull your pants down and lay face down on the table," the artist ordered. He pulled out the tools he would use to "brand" me. I pretended it wasn't happening. My body tingled and hurt as the drill of the tool bore into a sensitive area near my buttocks.

"It hurts." My body involuntary tensed.

"Just relax." Did I hear compassion in his voice?

I laid still and took it, willing my mind elsewhere.

After the tattoo was seared forever into my body, I hurried into the bathroom. I used a small mirror to see what had been put on my backside. I gasped. I saw the words *Property of T.W.* with an unrecognizable word in the crack of my butt. He'd also imprinted a pair of women's lips on either side and a rose under the initials.

Strangely, a sense of value spread over me. Thomas did still want me. He wanted me enough to make me his forever.

I smiled.

"Hey, Debbie, haven't seen you for a while." It was Darnell, and Darryl was with him.

They were my chance to escape. Running over to their car, I pleaded, "Help me! Thomas is holding me against my will."

They took me to my mother's house to hide. After several hours, I got up the nerve to walk to a donut shop nearby. Within minutes, Thomas walked through the door. My heart sank.

"Thomas, I'm so sorry. I'm sorry," I begged.

"Don't worry. Everything's fine. I care so much about you, baby. I was just concerned something bad happened to you." His voice oozed with an eerie niceness. "I want what's best for you. Come on. Let me take you to get some rest. You've had a long day." He took my hand and pulled me out of the shop.

"Okay." Several weeks had passed since he'd last hit me, so I hoped he wouldn't hurt me. He'd tattooed me to show how much he loved me, hadn't he?

But as soon as we got back to the motel room, he changed. Thomas closed the door, pushed me, and yelled into my face. "You—! What are you trying to do to me?" He kicked me and kicked and kicked while I tried to steady myself on a table. This went on for several minutes, but it seemed like hours. Miraculously none of my bones broke, but my body was badly bruised, and blood oozed from open wounds. He hadn't touched my face. Thomas left me to get in bed, where I stayed for several days—alone except for when he brought me food and water.

On another occasion, I escaped and found a fast food hamburger place. My stomach growled with hunger, and I didn't have money on me. I tried to get a date so I could eat, but Thomas found me. Again, he was nice until we got back to his room. This time, his anger exploded. Grabbing a hanger out of the closet, he beat me relentlessly on my hands, feet, and back. Screams escaped my mouth, but no one came to my rescue. Was there no one to help me?

Each lash burned into my skin and left imprints. But Thomas was always careful to protect my face. It took a week in bed to recover from my injuries.

How was Thomas always finding me? Was it Mom? My heart, soul, and body broke. During the time I lay recovering, I once again concluded the only way I could survive my predicament was to work harder than ever before. Debra Woods would do what needed to be done to gain and keep Thomas's confidence. I would do my job with a positive attitude and bring in as much money as I could. When I did, I would be treated well. I might not survive another beating.

We spent a lot of time in Fresno and made a great deal of money—or rather Thomas did. He kept me out into the early mornings. Once I'd regained his trust, I asked if I could get up and start early. My goal was to be in by eight at night. Every morning, I slid out of bed at six, showered, walked to a restaurant close by, ate, and brought Thomas back breakfast. He didn't have to tell me anything. I just did what I had to do with a smile on my face, even if I didn't feel it. My goal was to survive.

CHAPTER TWELVE

I came to despise cops. They always treated me with revulsion, calling me a slut and other degrading names. That is, everywhere but Fresno. The Fresno police showed me respect and acted like I was important. Especially one cop—Officer Fries.

Fries always smiled and looked me in the eye. "Are you all right, Debra?"

"I'm all right."

One night he asked me, "Why are you doing this, Debbie?"

"Because I want to."

"No one wants to be doing this."

"I do," I tried to make sure my confident tone assured him.

There was a gentle, almost godly, spirit about him. He reminded me of Grandma. I felt safe when he was around. I often jumped out in front of his car the moment I saw him on patrol. He'd greet me with a warm welcome, arrest me, and book me. The same night I'd be released. Thomas would pick me up and let me rest until the next day. I was arrested thirty-seven times in less than a year. Mostly to get off the streets. Mostly because of Officer Fries. He seemed to really care, but I couldn't trust him enough to tell him I needed help.

There were other kind souls out there. My heart was unusually heavy one night, but I put on a smile and walked out the door. As always, my goal was to keep Thomas happy until I could find a way to escape.

Cars drove by looking for women to pick up along an older, outdated motel strip close to Highway 99 in Fresno. Pimps rode in their late-model cars, watching what they considered their property. A middle-aged woman caught my attention. She appeared to be a nice lady, and she tried to talk to all of us working the street. Most of the girls ignored her, but I wanted to listen to what she had to say.

"Hello, my name is Jackie. May I pray with you?"

Pray with me? Why would this nice church-looking lady want to pray with me? I didn't deserve to be prayed for. Look at what I was doing, even if it wasn't by choice.

"I would love for you to pray for me," I told her.

"What is your name?"

"Debbie."

She took my hands. "Father, thank you for my sweet sister, Debbie. Thank you that you have allowed me to pray with her tonight. Lord, I ask you to bless her, show her your love, and watch over her. Lord, let her know what a special jewel she is and that you have a plan for her life. Amen."

A jewel? I'm a jewel? There's a plan for me?

She didn't judge or demean, which surprised me. We talked a bit more. I felt so comfortable with her. "Can I go home with you?" I asked.

"Honey, I wish I could take you home, but I can't." She hugged me.

My heart sank. She came to pray with me but offered no other help. Officer Fries seemed to want to help, but I doubted he could either. Maybe there was no help for a woman like me. Maybe, for me, this was all there was.

OFFICER FRIES

CHAPTER THIRTEEN

Officer Fries' Story

My parents provided a safe, happy, and supportive home. My father was a police officer and, eventually, a lieutenant, with the Fresno Police Department. Still, I never planned to become a police officer.

My parents didn't tolerate lying. They taught me to respect authority. At age nineteen, I married and became a father at twenty-one. To care for my family, I worked multiple jobs. Needing more money, I took the test to become a correctional officer at the Fresno County Jail, was hired, and found law enforcement was my calling.

I finished the police academy in 1998. At the age of twenty-six, I was sworn in as a rookie officer with the Fresno Police Department. I was following in my father's footsteps.

But my sheltered and moral upbringing did little to prepare me for what I would face on the job.

Like all new officers, I started out patrolling the streets. Two of my on-the-job training phases were spent in what was called, at that time, the Central District. The fast-paced area housed a diverse mash of cultures—drug users, sellers, and women who worked on the streets. It was not unusual to handle twenty or more calls a night during my ten-hour shift.

One of the first nights, my trainer and I answered a robbery call. A young delivery man told us he'd been robbed while delivering pizza. I immediately believed him. Pulling me aside, my mentor pointed out the inconsistencies in the story. He encouraged me to go back and confront the delivery man about the conflicts, which I did. I was shocked to realize that someone would flat out lie to me—a cop. It was clear that I needed to reevaluate the way I saw things.

Growing up, the ugliness of life escaped me, so it was hard to witness the heartbreaking realities. Every night, I ran across too much violence, too many broken families, too many eyes full of despair and hopelessness. I struggled to manage the emotions of what I experienced each night.

Each night brought something different. I fought to save the lives of overdose victims, stabbing victims, and shooting victims. I helped lost elderly men and women who'd walked away from their homes and held the hands of children with multiple, unexplained bruises. I brought comfort to people who'd been beaten over pocket change. The list of crimes and victims is long. Many nights were like a yo-yo, my heart breaking over and over. Like the night I answered a call to find a child who had suffocated between the bars of his bed. Then, on to neighbors arguing over a tree that bordered their properties. So many times, I wanted to scream, "Your problem is not important!" But I'd put on my professional demeanor and keep on.

Often, the only way I or anyone dealing with so much tragedy could survive was to turn off every emotion—to feel *nothing*. I couldn't escape the frequent nightmares I had in the first years on the job until I learned to go by the book—black and white. If you broke the law, you got in trouble. I studied the codes for every violation that would allow me to stop, contact, and arrest someone. There were no breaks given. This was the only way I could handle call after call, night after night.

When I encountered girls on the street, I was pleasant and encouraged them to feel safe and talk with me. They'd easily confess. I'd give them a warning to leave the area. If I saw them again, they would be arrested for loitering for the purpose of prostitution. No breaks. It was illegal, and that was that.

In the late nineties, the general feeling of law enforcement and the public was that the girls were out there by choice. They liked making fast and easy money, and there was a lot to be made. But they were breaking the law, and it was my job to enforce it.

One night, that all changed.

♦ ♦ ♦

May 1999

Betty was about forty-five years old, but she looked sixty-five. She was addicted to crack cocaine and sold herself to make the money she needed to support her habit. For some reason, Betty trusted me. She was on a form of probation called S.O.A.P (Stay Out of the Area of Prostitution). She often broke the rules of her probation, so I repeatedly arrested her for loitering with the intent to prostitute. It got to the point where I'd just pull up and say, "Get in the car." Betty would open the back door, get in, and I would drive her to the station.

I became curious about why Betty was on the streets. Since I had gained her trust, one day I asked her about it.

"What can I do to help get you off the streets?"

"There's nothin' you can do. This is my life."

Why would someone *choose* this life?

"What's your story, Betty?"

"Do you really wanna know?"

"Yes, I would."

Betty told me a story that would forever change my perspective.

"I was raised here in Fresno," she started. "My whole life, my mother was a prostitute who brought her customers to our apartment. She was a drug addict and paid little attention to me, until one night when Mom brought a man home. I was just fifteen years old." Her breath caught before she continued. "He looked at me and told my mother he would pay double. Without skipping a beat, my mother glared at me and said, 'Go into the bedroom with the nice gentleman.'" A tear slipped from Betty's eye as she recounted the night her mother betrayed her.

My heart broke as she described her life. I listened with a sense of realization and shame that perhaps Betty's lifestyle was not her fault. Her account shook me, forcing me to think deeply about how I'd viewed girls working on the street. How many women were crying out for help and I hadn't noticed? How many were prisoners to their circumstances? What could I do to help them? Those were the questions that kept me up at night.

I needed to know the women's *true* stories. Betty was the first to tell me her story, but she'd not be the last. No matter how painful it might be, I committed myself to seek out and listen to the women I encountered each night. Their stories horrified me. The father who sold his young daughter to men in the middle of the night. Each night, she'd fall asleep, terrified, never knowing if she might be awakened. The mother who walked out on her kids, leaving them to fend for themselves each day while she used men to make ends meet, then used drugs to calm the shame. And there were so many more like this. Time after time I listened as they explained, "I *can't* leave."

I felt helpless and didn't believe there was anything I could do to help these women. How could the problem be fixed? There seemed to be no answer. What was the problem? I had no idea. I just knew in my heart that none of the girls could possibly, truly, deep down, want to be out on the street selling themselves. The hopelessness in their eyes validated my feelings.

Betty and the other women I had conversations with changed the way I saw those who walked the streets. A realization hit me. These women are not criminals; they are victims.

Debra Woods was one of the first women I came across after my change in perspective.

♦ ♦ ♦

There was something about her. Something *different*.

Debra was pleasant and always seemed happy to see me. The two of us built a comfortable relationship. She told me about her hopes and dreams, but nothing big. She couldn't grasp what she could become.

When I would stop her, always in high prostitution areas, we would chat. "Debra, let me help you get off the streets," I asked more than once.

Her answers were always the same: "No. I'm out here by choice. This is the way I make my living."

How could she be telling the truth? How could she choose to live this way?

I arrested Debra too many times to count. I wanted her off the streets and was willing to do whatever it took. She was smart and had so much potential. Her dreams should've been much bigger than they were.

There never was a time when I felt Debra wanted to accept my offer of help, but we both knew the truth. Help for women involved in this illegal activity were minimal or nonexistent. All I really had to offer was friendship.

Then, suddenly, Debra disappeared. But I never forgot her...

CHAPTER FOURTEEN

Debra

The more money I made for Thomas, the more he left me alone, and the more he praised me. My youthfulness and good looks made it easy for me to pick up dates and ask for top dollar. Some days, Thomas brought me in after my quota for that day and let me smoke weed. It allowed me to escape my reality. When I was compliant, he left me alone.

Thomas began to trust me. I cheerfully did what he wanted and brought in $5,000 a day. I turned over all I earned without blinking an eye. He fed me well and made sure I had something to take so I could sleep. In Los Angeles, I was considered high-class—a high-class date. He kept me in nice clothes and drug-free, except for a little weed and sleeping pills. My best motivation was the praise Thomas showered on me. "You're making me rich. You're good."

I beamed with pride. There is no denying, I relished the approval and special privileges. Sometimes he gave me a day off or let me call my son, though he listened in on my conversations. So, I always spoke with an upbeat voice.

"Get in the bathroom," Thomas ordered. "I have friends coming, and we have business to discuss."

Sitting on the floor by the door, I listened to Thomas and the others talking.

"My girl brought in $1,000 last night," one said.

"My girl brought in $2,500," another bragged.

"My Little Debbie brought in $5,000. She brings in at least $5,000 every night." Thomas's tone was filled with pride.

"No way."

Outperforming the other girls is what kept me safe and cared for. But why did Thomas have to shut me in the bathroom? It was like a cell. Hadn't I earned his trust?

"I swear, you messed up with this girl. She is gonna send you to prison," I heard one of the other pimps say to Thomas. The words puzzled me. Why did his friend say such a thing? I thought it was because I wouldn't be Thomas's girlfriend, but he'd made it clear we weren't in a romantic relationship. While other pimps had a girl they called their girlfriend, Thomas rented rooms with two beds. He was not ever planning to be my boyfriend. We had a partnership. That was all.

Well, a partnership where I took all the risk and Thomas took all the money.

I heard conversations such as, "I broke my girl's nose last night. She's not going to run," and other stories of abuse on the girls they pimped.

Thomas recruited other young women, but they didn't last long. He expected them to bring in as much money as I did, but they couldn't.

He probably sold them.

Most of the time things went well. A date picked me up, paid me, we did our thing, and I moved to the next. Sometimes it was more dangerous. Standing on the street one night, I watched as a dark vehicle pulled up.

"You're beautiful. How much?" the handsome dark man behind the wheel asked.

He seemed nice enough. I was tired and wanted to get my quota for the night. Something stirred in my soul that this might not be good. It would be okay, I decided. "Two hundred," I said, flirting.

He opened the door for me from his side, making me feel safe. But things changed quickly. In a flash, his personality switched. An agitated look came over his face, his eyes turning red. His voice changed from friendly, to disturbed, to angry, using language I cannot write.

I was in trouble. I quickly pulled my pepper spray from my purse and sprayed him in the face. The mist had no effect, except to make him angrier. Wiping his eyes as if he was rubbing off water, he berated, "You messed up. Tonight, you're going to die."

I found the door handle of the fast-moving vehicle and opened the door, falling out onto a busy highway. I don't remember what happened next, but I woke up in the hospital with a road rash on my arms, legs, and face, which kept me there a few days—a welcome rest. Thomas came to see me, even brought flowers, but when I got back to the hotel, he beat me for not following the rules. "Breaking the rules cost me money, girl."

What rule?

Still I stayed loyal.

Thomas trusted me to be on my own. I was addicted to his praise, and there was no way to escape anyway. On one occasion, at two in the morning, it was quiet on the street. There were no other girls around. They had all finished for the night. A red sports car pulled up. The guy looked kind of cute but appeared to have been drinking. He gave me payment up front and ordered me to sit on my hands, which I did—another broken rule. The door was locked, and the windows were up. He started to drive in the direction of the Hollywood mountains.

"You want to know a secret?" he asked, looking straight ahead.

"Sure." I turned my head toward him.

"See those hills?"

I looked in that direction as he pulled over to the side of the road.

"I've killed a lot of girls like you."

He had my attention.

"They're buried in those hills. Maybe tonight you'll join them."

Panic rose within me and immediately I started to pray silently. *God help me. God help me.* When I tried to turn the handle, the door wouldn't budge—I was trapped.

Then something caught my eye to the right. The door seemed to fly open. I jumped out, fell onto the soft grass between the road and the sidewalk, and sat there, but not before I caught the terrified look on the man's face. Whoever or whatever he saw scared him so badly, he put the car in gear and sped off.

Relieved, I looked around, but no one was there. Who had opened the door? I picked myself up, found a pay phone, and called Thomas. I told him what had happened, but he didn't care.

I thought of Grandma. I missed her.

CHAPTER FIFTEEN

1999

A black, late-model sports car pulled up. Inside, a dark man smiled back at me. His accent told me he was a foreigner—not uncommon in Los Angeles, California.

"How much?"

The car he drove and his expensive clothes implied that he had money and lots of it. "Two hundred."

"Come on. Get in." He leaned over to open my door.

Reaching for the door handle, I slid into the leather seat beside him, taking in the scent of his over-powering cologne. "I need to take the money up front."

He ignored me.

He's good for it. I'll ask again when we get where we're going.

We made our way to his upscale hotel room. He closed the door and began to undress. "Strip," he demanded. His tone frightened me, and he'd still not paid.

"I need the money first." Something wasn't right. What was this guy's deal?

Laughing, he stood over me, raised his right hand and slapped me across the face. A scream escaped my lips.

I thought of Andrew.

The man grabbed my shoulders and slammed my body onto the king size bed. Determined to escape, I fought with all my strength. He was strong and quickly overpowered me. Silently and avoiding my eyes, he tugged at my blouse, tearing it off. He lifted me from the bed and ripped off my pants, taking what he wanted without using a condom. He raped me, which may sound funny, considering what I did every day, but this was different. I felt violated. But I had a police record. I knew no one would care, even if I could tell them what happened. I took what he dished out, simply to survive.

"Get out of here," he yelled when he was through, not giving me time to catch my breath.

Struggling, I pulled myself together as best I could. I ran down the stairs instead of using the elevator, which emptied into the parking garage. I found a phone and called Thomas.

"You messed up. You messed up, girl. You're supposed to collect the money first," Thomas screamed. He wasn't listening and didn't care. "Now I have to come and get you."

After Thomas picked me up and took me back to the hotel room, I took a hot shower. Sobbing, I fell on my knees, water dripping from my hair. I had to find a way out.

A few weeks later, something started to change in my body. My breasts felt tender. I woke up feeling sick to my stomach. I couldn't keep food down.

"You got the flu?" Thomas appeared worried.

"Probably," I replied, but I wondered if something else was wrong.

When I skipped my period the second month, I suspected I might be pregnant and confirmed it with a pregnancy test bought with money Thomas gave me. I kept my secret to myself, even though feelings of hopelessness fell over me. After coming in one night, I went straight to bed and begged to be left alone. I forced myself to get up the next morning—I knew Thomas wouldn't have it. My mind was full of worry and confusion. There was only one way out—I'd have to end my life.

Lying in bed thinking of how I might kill myself, something inside of me clicked. One minute my heart was filled with dread and the next hope. I didn't understand then where the thought came from. In an instant, I decided I wasn't going to live that way anymore. I wasn't going to die there.

I devised a plan to escape. One that would require great risk.

A middle-aged man wearing dark-rimmed glasses drove up and asked, "How much?" He seemed nervous but nice.

We agreed on a price before I got in his car.

"What's your name?"

No one ever asked my name. "Debbie."

We exchanged small talk as we drove toward his hotel. For a moment, I thought he might be a cop. I prayed he wasn't one of Thomas's men checking on me. "I need your help," I blurted out before I could change my mind. "My boyfriend is dangerous, and I don't know what to do. I can't take it anymore. Do what you want to me, but please help me."

The man listened.

I waited anxiously for his answer.

After a long pause, he turned to me with sincerity on his face. "I'll help you, and I'm not going to touch you. I don't want you to do anything against your will. What do you need?"

"I need to get to Fresno. Can you take me to catch a bus? I have no money."

"I'll take care of it. Don't worry." His voice reassured me.

He drove me to the bus station and paid my fare. He put both the ticket and a twenty-dollar bill in my hand and waited until the bus pulled up. We didn't have to wait long. I gave my rescuer a quick hug. "Thank you."

"Take care of yourself." He stood watching until the bus drove away.

I found a seat in the back, hoping to hide. Luckily, it was a cold night. My blue velour pant set kept me warm and didn't advertise to the world what I didn't want known.

Thomas trusted me. I made sure of that, if for no other reason than to stay in his good graces and to keep from being beaten. But I knew sometimes he watched me. "To protect my assets," he'd say.

At each stop from Los Angeles to Fresno, my stomach churned. I was terrified he would walk on and drag me off. In the wee hours of the morning, the bus pulled up to the terminal in downtown Fresno. I shuddered, as the thought that Thomas might be there floated through my mind. When I stepped out into the wet, cold, foggy morning, I quickly checked my surroundings. There was no Thomas, only homeless men huddled close to the building, trying to keep warm.

CHAPTER SIXTEEN

I exhaled a sigh of relief that Thomas wasn't there to greet me, then my thoughts turned to the man who'd helped me escape. I was grateful he had helped me, but now I had to figure out what was next. I couldn't trust Mom, but she was the only one I knew to call. I'd burned my bridges with Daddy, I thought, and there was no one else.

"The police are looking for you," Mom told me. "They've come asking for you several times." Mom handed me the stack of warrants, mostly for solicitation of prostitution and failing to show up for court. Each time I was arrested, I'd given her address.

It occurred to me that jail would be the safest place for me. "Mom, I'm going to turn myself in. Will you go with me?" Mother agreed and went with me to the county jail. She stayed by my side, like a protective mother hen. "I am so proud of you, Debbie. I could never be brave enough to do that." Mom said, beaming with pride. Her words disgusted me, but I kept silent.

Inside, I seethed. *You are the reason I am here!* How could this be a conversation a mother and daughter were having? Was I getting a gold star here? Was she proud of me? Proud of *what*?

"May I help you?" A uniformed woman asked.

"I'm here to turn myself in."

"Your full name?" Her monotone voice said she was all business.

"Debra Carol Woods."

She typed my name in the computer. "Wait here, please." When she returned a few minutes later, two officers accompanied her.

One read my rights while the other handcuffed me before they escorted me to a holding cell for processing. I was relieved. I was in no hurry to get out.

"Carol Woods," the bailiff called.

"Carol Woods," she called again.

I didn't answer right away. She looked straight at me and announced again, "*Carol Woods.*"

"That's not my name. My name is Debra Woods."

"Let me see your bracelet." The bailiff checked my wrist. "Carol Woods. That's what your bracelet says. Congratulations. You have a new alias."

In 2000, anyone looking to find an inmate needed to know the exact name they'd been processed under. Carol was my middle name, but Thomas had never asked. He only knew me as Debra or Little Debbie. He hadn't bothered to find out much about me, except my weaknesses. Was this a sign or just a stroke of good luck?

A few days later, I went to court. Due to a large number of warrants for my arrest, the judge gave me 180 days in jail. I couldn't have been happier. Just what I needed. Jail would be a lot better than living under the thumb of Thomas and his abuse. It would give me time to be safe and figure out where to go from here.

I contacted Daddy, fully expecting him to chastise me, but I had to try. I really needed him now.

"Carol Woods, you have a visitor," I heard over the loudspeaker. In a rush of excitement, I went to see who was waiting.

"Daddy! Grandma! It's so good to see you!" I ached to crawl into Daddy's arms and have him hold me, but a sheet of glass separated us.

After answering my questions about Andrew, Daddy looked at me tenderly. "How are you doing, honey?" Emotion built up inside of me as I poured out my story. I told them everything.

"You're not going to believe me, but this is not my fault. Thomas tricked me into going to Los Angles with him. He held me against my will. I just wanted to survive." I told them the details of trying to escape and the beatings I endured. When I mentioned the man who threatened to kill me, Grandma got a strange look on her face.

"What time did that happen, Debbie?" Grandma asked.

"About two in the morning. Why?"

"Do you know the date?"

"In November."

Grandma looked stunned. "It must have been the night I woke up around two a.m. I knew something was horribly wrong. The Holy Spirit prompted me to get on my knees and pray for you." Grandma held her hand over her heart and spoke quietly. "I felt that you were in some kind of trouble. I begged the Lord to protect you. Then a peace came over me, and I knew you were all right."

Tears streamed down her face and mine.

"Grandma, I always thought of you and your prayers." I sniffled.

"Why didn't you tell me, Debra. "You're my daughter. I would have helped you." Daddy pressed his hand against the window. A tear rolled over his cheek.

"I didn't think you or anyone would believe me," I cried.

All three of us were a teary, happy mess, but my stomach churned in anticipation of what I had to reveal. Getting up the courage, I took a deep breath. "I have one more thing. My pregnancy test was positive. I don't know who the father is."

"My baby." Daddy's voice hushed as his eyes filled with love. "It will all work out."

I was speechless. I clenched my right fist over my heart then extended it to Daddy in a show of gratitude. He was a gift from God.

"Thank you for coming. Thank you for believing me. I love you so much." It was time for our visit to end.

Grandma and Daddy told me they loved me, but I already knew, because they came, listened, and believed me. Feeling much lighter, I bounced back to my cell, the ton of bricks lifted from my shoulders.

I tried to pretend I wasn't pregnant. Maybe if I didn't think about the baby growing inside me, it would go away. But at three months, my pregnancy could no longer be hidden. My plan was to put my baby up for adoption—or abortion might be easier. I didn't know anything about the father, other than that he was dark, a foreigner. The one who raped me. When Grandma visited, I told her of my decision to either adopt or abort.

Grandma looked horrified. "No, you can't! I'll care for the baby."

"I'll pray about it, Grandma. I promise."

On my walk back to my cell, I felt a spirit stir within me. I couldn't abort my baby.

That night, I prayed like I'd promised. *God if you get me out of jail before the baby is born, I will keep it. If I am still in jail, I will give the baby up for adoption.*

My decision was made, but my heart yearned for my son, whom I hadn't had contact with for over a year. I didn't want him to see me for the first time with a new baby in my arms. I didn't want him to think I loved the new baby more.

CHAPTER SEVENTEEN

On the seventh day, they got up at daybreak and marched around the city seven times in the same manner, except that on that day they circled the city seven times.

(JOSHUA 6:15)

The Fresno County Jail stands six stories high. At that time, men were housed on the third, fourth, and fifth, floors, and the women on the sixth. Each level had two tiers of cells. The roof was the exercise area and where inmates could get a breath of fresh air each day. It was the size of a basketball court and was broken up into areas separating men and women.

I attended all the chapel and church services offered in jail. It didn't take long before they recognized me as a spiritual leader among the other inmates. Miss Martin, one of the correctional officers, played an essential role in encouraging me to stay strong. She handed out inspirational messages written on pieces of paper. They lifted my spirits. In my teenage years, I'd turned my back on God. But now I needed Him.

I discussed my dilemma about the baby with Miss Martin. "Pray about it before you make your decision," she counseled.

"I will. I promise."

Three months after I was sentenced, ladies from a local church invited the inmates to walk around the exercise area on the roof seven times, like Joshua in the Bible. The church ladies would pace around the outside of the building at the same time. We were asked to pray as we walked, to break the chains of spiritual barriers over the jail. Quick to volunteer, I encouraged others to walk with me.

Thanks to Miss Martin, who let us out onto the court, we started our laps early in the morning. There were more than twenty women who started, but only three of us finished. The others dropped out as we marched around and around and around—seven times. We were on a spiritual high. We sang and praised God. I was uplifted but tired at the end. I went back to my bunk and drifted into a deep, peaceful sleep.

"Carol Woods," I heard over the loudspeaker. The screechy blare startled me awake. "Can you be rolled up in three minutes?"

"Yes," I yelled back, once I was fully awake.

Shaking, I got my stuff together. Where was I going? The two girls who'd finished the walk with me had been called too. Together, we went to the guard station.

Miss Martin met us there. "You three are being released tonight. We need to process you."

A smile spread across our faces as we heard joyous clapping and yelling from those who would be left behind.

"I'm going to keep my baby, Miss Martin."

Tears welled in her eyes as she patted me on the shoulder. I grasped her hand.

"Thank you for everything."

CHAPTER EIGHTEEN

Daddy picked me up at midnight, just like he said he would. Wrapped in his arms, I felt safe and loved. He told me about his plan to help me and keep me from whoever meant me harm.

Daddy and my family planned for me to leave Fresno and live in Sacramento. Mom wasn't told.

All I could think of on the ride home was seeing Andrew, my now four-year-old son. As soon as Daddy stopped the car in his driveway, I opened the door and ran up the steps into the house to find my boy. I tiptoed into his room.

He woke up the moment I kissed him.

"Mommy!" He grinned when I got in bed. It felt so good to hold him and feel the weight of his small body next to me. We fell asleep together, safe and secure in each other's arms.

At six the next morning, the pickup was loaded and ready to go. Andrew's things were packed with mine. We left for Sacramento, where Daddy had arranged for me to stay with my cousin. I couldn't believe I could have my son. "Andrew needs to be with his Mommy," Daddy assured me.

We enjoyed the ride to Sacramento together, but as much as my son was happy to see his mother, it was clear he loved Papa more. When Andrew saw Daddy unload the truck, he cried, "No, Papa." As Daddy drove away, Andrew wailed, "Take me, take me."

He sobbed himself to sleep that first night.

Guilt filled my heart. What was I doing to my son? He had always been with his Papa.

The next morning, my son was a little down, but glad to be with Mommy.

It was close to the birth of my second child, but I stayed well disconnected from the life growing inside me. I didn't want to know if it was a girl or boy. Secretly, I was still considering adoption.

♦ ♦ ♦

"It's a girl," the doctor announced.

The moment I saw my daughter, every doubt about keeping her faded. My heart overflowed with love as I gazed into the face of my beautiful baby with her dark complexion. Her brown eyes matched her thick, dark hair. I named her Kiara Renae. I was no longer angry at the john who raped me. He'd given me this beautiful gift.

I drifted off into a peaceful sleep, but not before saying a prayer. "Thank You for giving me this precious daughter."

Early the next morning, I woke up with the worst headache of my life. I was sure a big rig had hit me. A pounding ran through the front and back of my head and spread downward through my neck. I couldn't lift my head. I was sick to my stomach, and it was impossible to move. *What's wrong with me?* Somehow, I managed to push the button by my side for help.

My dura, which is the thick, outermost layer of membrane enveloping the brain and spinal cord, had ruptured. A small amount of spinal fluid had leaked out. I spent the next week in the hospital with my family at my side. A week later, the headaches finally subsided. When I went home, Grandma took care of my babies and me until I was stronger. Just like Daddy, I could always count on Grandma.

I needed to support my growing family. Public assistance wasn't enough, and it wasn't what I wanted for my life. A month after Kiara was born, I went to work at a local pizza parlor. I learned quickly how to toss a pizza. In a matter of a few months, I became the shift manager and was soon promoted to a manager over several stores. Everything seemed to be going well, until one day, a familiar looking man came into the shop.

I suddenly felt sick to my stomach.

I could hear Thomas in my head as if he were in the room. *Don't mess with me.* My body felt the pain of the beatings.

"*Noooo!*" I wailed.

"What's wrong?" my co-worker asked. "You look like you've seen a ghost."

"Can you wait on him?" I quickly ran to hide in the back of the store—my heart racing. I stood there, wringing my sweaty hands, taking a few minutes to calm myself.

I didn't know the man standing at the counter. He hadn't tried to harm me, but I'd still had a physical reaction. And it wasn't the last time something like that happened. Those voices spoke in my head every time I saw a man who resembled one of the men who'd abused and betrayed me.

Why was this happening? Wasn't I safe?

Still, something wasn't right. I'd managed to escape the horrors of Thomas but could not escape the memories of the trauma I'd endured.

Hiding my fear as best I could, I moved on with life and settled into an apartment with my kids. My new neighbors, Ruby and Frank, introduced themselves to me right away and even helped me move in.

"We're having a few friends over tonight. Why don't you join us?" Ruby asked.

"I have my kids. I can't," I said, with a bit of disappointment.

"If you change your mind, come on over."

I stayed home that night, but a week later I was invited again. Needing some social interaction, I decided, why not. What harm would it be if I snuck over after Andrew and Kiara were asleep? I'd be just next door. After the kids were tucked snuggly in bed, I left my apartment and knocked on my neighbors' door.

"Debbie! Come in and meet our friends." Ruby grinned with delight.

Friends weren't all I met.

I soon found out I lived next door to drug addicts. I was a perfect target. Over the next few weeks, I would be offered—and gladly tried—cocaine, weed, and whatever else they had.

"Try this, Debbie," Frank said, offering me something new.

"What's that?"

"Just a little meth. Try it."

In the instant after I snorted meth for the first time, everything changed. My heart raced and beat faster, and then faster. I grew ten feet tall. In my reality, I became stronger and more courageous, beyond what I'd ever felt. I was not afraid of anything or anyone. That included Thomas.

Drugs helped me forget the shame and guilt I carried. They helped me forget my children. I began to separate myself from them. They were no longer important. I didn't give a second thought to leaving them by themselves.

My meth habit affected my job. I didn't get to work on time and sometimes didn't show up at all. It didn't take long to get myself fired. With my job gone, I had to get a new one. Dancing was what I knew, so I hired someone to watch my kids, and off I went. Youth and beauty still favored me, and the money was good.

One night a tall, dark, and handsome man approached me after a dance. "Can I buy you a drink?"

"Sure." I fluttered my eyes.

But he had other things on his mind. After the bar waitress brought our drinks and after a little flirting, he took my hands and hit me with a proposal: "I'll give you a thousand dollars to spend the night with me."

Hesitating for a moment, I diverted my eyes to the floor. I needed the money to buy drugs, so I looked back up at him and said, "I'd love to."

Geared for self-preservation, I chose the profession I knew best. The difference was, I was choosing it. No one was forcing me now. I was getting the money I made—not Thomas or any other pimp. And the drugs numbed me, so I didn't feel sorry about my decision.

♦ ♦ ♦

No one ever talked to me about what I was doing or tried to stop me. They never, ever said I was a victim or tried to help.

I heard the whispers behind my back: *She's choosing to do this.* And I believed them. I needed to survive. I *always* needed to survive.

My whole life was soon focused on how to pay for my next hit. I quit paying my bills. Before long, I received an eviction notice from my apartment manager. Even though my brother and I hadn't been close through the years, I called him, in hopes he would allow me to stay with him.

"No. Dad always bails you out, but I'm not going to." He sounded angry. That door was shut.

I hung up the phone, not knowing what to do. I thought about calling Daddy, but a knock interrupted me. When I opened the door, I couldn't believe my eyes. "Nelson! When did you get out of prison?"

Nelson wanted to take me back to Fresno, but I was afraid of encountering Thomas. "I can't go back."

"Yes, you can."

"No, he will find me."

"He's not a factor anymore."

I wasn't sure what that meant, but I figured that somehow Nelson had found out about Thomas and had a "talk" with him. Nelson once again protected me. He helped me buy a gun and taught me how to use it. I needed to defend myself and survive. There was only one way I knew to do that.

CHAPTER NINETEEN

A few days later, I agreed to let Nelson help me. He drove me, six-year-old Andrew, and one-year-old Kiera to Daddy's house. Andrew jumped out of the car as soon as we pulled into the driveway.

"Papa!" he screamed, running into his grandfather's arms. Daddy pulled him up to his chest and held him tightly, an obvious happy reunion.

Daddy kissed Kiara and then hugged me. "I'm glad to see you."

He let us move in with him and his wife. They were not thrilled to be getting three new houseguests. However, Daddy allowed me to stay until things got better. Of course, the kids weren't all I brought into their home. I also carried a secret that Dad did not detect—my drug addiction. At least I told myself he didn't see it.

After the new year, my first ever income tax refund made it possible for me to move with my kids into a new apartment. But before long, I was evicted—again—for not paying rent. Drugs ruled my life and were more important than a roof over our heads, food, or my children. Nelson tried to get me to stop, but I didn't care. Life was too hard. Drugs allowed me to feel nothing, covering the pain of my guilt and anxieties.

I reconnected with an old friend, Maurice, who sold high-quality marijuana. We spent a lot of time partying. The profession I knew best supplemented my income, but I soon realized I was pregnant again. Nelson ecstatically believed the baby was his, but I was sure it was Maurice's. It was too risky to tell Nelson the truth, though. I couldn't bear to see Maurice meet the same fate as Dutch and Ted had a few years earlier.

Despite my wretched life, I protected my children as best I could. Andrew lived with his Papa, and I had Kiara. This new baby would make three. Somehow, when I carried another human being inside of me, my will was strong. During these times, I put my baby above drugs. However, I was still on the streets.

Eight months pregnant, homeless, and with no place to go, I drove, with my daughter, to the Marjorie Mason Center in downtown Fresno. It was a safe house founded in the name of a woman who'd died at the hands of her abusive husband. In the early morning hours, I knocked on the door seeking help. The lady who answered the door agreed to hear my story. I described being kidnapped, forced to sleep with men, and the beatings. I told her about Thomas as if I had just escaped. In my reality, I decided I had.

"I need to get away from him and be safe."

Looking at my belly, the lady beckoned us, "Come in."

I held Kiara on my lap and answered her questions. She took Kiara and me to a large bedroom and suggested we go to sleep. Exhausted from the late hour, I fell into bed and was asleep before my head hit my pillow.

It was close to the time of my second daughter's birth. During my last exam, the doctor felt my stomach. A look of concern covered his face, which caused me to be anxious. "We're going to look at your baby."

A nurse helped me onto a gurney and rolled me into the ultrasound room. The image on the screen revealed the umbilical cord wrapped around her neck. I watched my baby struggle, but there was nothing I could do.

God save my baby, I prayed. An ambulance rushed me to the hospital, where I was prepped for a Caesarean section. A few hours later, November 20, 2001, Juliana was born. I instantly fell in love—again.

The doctor released Juliana and me a few days later. We went back to the Marjorie Mason Center. With a new baby and a two-year-old to care for, I felt overwhelmed and alone. Even though Daddy came to see me in the hospital, I was now on my own, except for the help and nurturing of the staff. My sweet Kiara assisted me with Juliana as best a toddler could. She became good at handing me diapers. Fortunately, I healed quickly.

Thirty days was the limit for residents to stay at Marjorie Mason. However, I was accepted into their transition home. I once again tried to put the pieces of my life back together, but the loneliness was more than I could bear. Often, I cried for what seemed like no reason. I couldn't stop myself. It took only a few weeks before I found the meth I needed to mask the pain. The pain of being alone with my nightmares.

Juliana had just turned two months old when she suddenly went stiff in my arms. Her legs and arms pushed out, her face turned blue, and she struggled to breathe.

"Help!" I screamed to the house manager. "My baby can't breathe."

"Call 911!" the Marjorie Mason house manager yelled. She grabbed Juliana and cleared her throat, allowing her to cry and breathe, before the paramedics arrived. It wasn't until we got to the hospital that I understood what was wrong.

"Juliana has Respiratory Syncytial Virus or RSV. It's a common virus that infects the lungs and breathing passages," the doctor explained. "It's especially dangerous for Juliana. She is so young. Her lungs are paper thin, and mucus is building up."

"Will she be all right?" What the doctor told me sounded scary.

"We're going to keep her in the hospital and hope for the best," he assured me. "We'll take good care of her, Mom."

Juliana improved after five days in the hospital but took a sudden plunge on the sixth day. Miraculously she pulled through. Before I took her home, back to the transitional house, I needed to learn how to care for her, which included learning Cardiopulmonary Resuscitation (CPR). I lost sleep worrying about Juliana. What if I didn't get to her in time if she had another attack? What if she were to die? Would there be anyone to help us next time?

Since the shelter doors locked behind us after six each evening, I propped open the back entrance when I stepped outside to take the garbage out, so I'd be able to get back in. When I returned, the door had been closed.

"Who shut that? Open the door!"

No one came.

Juliana and Kiara were alone in our room.

Juliana could stop breathing. I must get to my babies. Juliana could die.

"Open the door! Open the door!" Picking up pebbles, I threw them at the windows. "Help me!"

Still no response.

I was now in a state of panic and pounded the door forcefully. Finally, one of the girls opened the door.

"What's wrong?"

I ran right past her, my mind wild with rage. I knew exactly who shut the door. Marci did, and she'd done it on purpose.

Marci and I had not gotten along since she arrived. We instantly took a disliking to one another, and that hadn't changed. I ran into my girls' room first. Finding them sleeping peacefully, I stomped down the hall to Marci's room.

"You shut the door on purpose." I wagged my finger at her.

"No, I didn't." She stepped away from me.

"You lie! You're not getting away with this." I lunged toward her, grabbed her hair and tugged. She didn't fight back but yelled for me to stop.

The resident manager walked into the room. She pulled me off her.

"*What* is going on?"

The next morning, Kiara, Juliana, and I were on the streets. I risked calling Daddy, in hopes he would come and rescue me. He showed up an hour later and took us home.

"I'm so disappointed in you. When are you going to get yourself together? You have three kids who need you." The sadness in Daddy's eyes sent a pang of guilt into my heart. "You can stay with me for a week, but you need to find your own way."

He was right. I didn't like who I'd become, but I didn't know how to stop.

At the time, Mom managed some less-than-perfect apartments. One unit sat empty, which Mom rented to me. I had very little money coming in. It was never enough to pay the expenses for me and to support my kids *and* my drug habit.

CHAPTER TWENTY

I started doing a little weed with Shawn, an old friend. He taught me more about meth, plunging me into a deeper addiction. I became an angrier person and not pleasant to be around. I didn't care about anything or anyone. I needed money and came up with an idea that would make me a lot of cash.

Thomas had taught me well, but I didn't need a pimp to sell my body. "A real professional can catch a date anywhere. She can turn any man into a trick," a friend on the street used to say. I came to believe that was indeed the truth.

My primary targets were older men. I would do what I needed to do to drain them of as much money as I could. Over time, I gathered names and phone numbers of my "dates" and recorded them in my little black book. The list grew to several hundred names. When I needed money, I just picked a number, called it, saw my client, and came away with enough to get me through to the next time. It was my job. I did it for money. It's how I survived. I'm not that bad, I told myself.

Shawn supplied me with drugs. Meth was my drug of choice because of the feelings of *I can do anything I want; nothing can touch me.* Meth also made me paranoid and bitter, plunging me into fits of uncontrolled anger that grew stronger over time.

I was a professional. I did what I needed to do to make sure my clients were happy and called back. The older the man, the more money he gave me. One eighty-year-old client was particularly generous. He was lonely, and I was happy to be his companion—for a price.

Shawn and I had an understanding. He had a couple of girlfriends on the side, which proved dangerous. One learned he was wanted by the United States Marshals. She didn't like the fact that other women were in his life, so she did what any unhappy girlfriend would do—she turned him in.

I was on my own again and evicted from our apartment because of the illegal activity. Luckily, one of my regulars, a wealthy businessman, owned several apartment buildings in town and allowed me to rent from him. I was happy to have a place to live.

♦ ♦ ♦

I answered the knock on my door. It was Nelson. It hadn't taken him long to find me once he was released from prison—again. Nelson was ready to come back into my life and be my protector. He still didn't like my drug habit but didn't try to stop me.

Soon after Nelson returned, I became pregnant. Once again, I didn't know who the father might be and decided it was Nelson's. As was my commitment, I quit using drugs. I let Nelson take care of me.

Gas and electricity were included in the rent I paid. And there was a reason for that. When an inspection was done on the apartment, it was discovered that the gas and electricity were illegally hooked up. The inspector had other suspicions too—suspicions of Nelson and me. Child Protective Services showed up and forced me to take a urine and hair sample to test for drugs. Of course, I came back clean. I was pregnant.

On July 7, 2003, Kendra, another beautiful girl, was born. After her birth, I had my tubes tied. Two toddlers and a newborn were more than I could deal with.

A fog of depression seeped into my mind. I felt lonelier and sadder than ever before. When I felt especially unhappy, I'd reach out to Mom. She didn't live too far away, and she'd invite me over to visit. I'd pack up my triple stroller and off we'd go.

CHAPTER TWENTY-ONE

Mom had married Jeff—husband number four. They had much in common: both loved drugs and both were ex-inmates. One afternoon, I answered the phone to the most blood-curdling sound I had ever heard. "Debra! Debra! Come quick. Something has happened to Jeff!" Mom's voice sounded panicked.

"What?"

"I think he's dead," she sobbed. "I think he's dead."

"Call 911. I'll be right there." I called a neighbor, asked her to watch my girls, and ran the two blocks to Mom's place. Before I got there, I heard sirens screaming.

I found Mom hunched over Jeff. "He's dying." Mom cried hysterically.

The paramedics wanted to transport him to the hospital right away.

"*Noooo*," Mom wailed.

"You have to let these men help him," I said, and pulled her off Jeff. Before the ambulance left, we were already in the car and on our way.

Jeff died the next day from blood poisoning. Years of pushing drugs and cocaine into his system had caught up with him. Jeff's family blamed Mom for his death and asked her to stay away from his funeral, despite her being his wife.

Mom couldn't bear her heartbreak. She was all alone, and she quickly fell deep into hopelessness, unable to sleep, eat, or function.

Less than two weeks after Jeff passed, I tried to call Mom. She didn't answer the phone. I kept trying but no luck. After loading my girls in their stroller, we headed over to Mom's place at a brisk pace. I knocked. No one answered. I peered through the window and immediately knew something was terribly wrong.

I used my key to open the door, and my worst fears were confirmed. Mom lay slumped on the floor, drug paraphernalia scattered around her. I called 911. I tried to wake her by shaking her arms and gently slapping her face.

"Leave me alone."

"Mom!" I shook her again.

"I have nothing to live for."

"Yes, you do."

When the paramedics arrived, they assessed their patient and strongly suggested she go to the hospital.

"No! I want to die."

"Please, let them take you to the hospital." I swallowed my tears.

"No!"

Since Mom wouldn't cooperate, there was nothing they could do. The paramedics left without her, but I knew she needed help.

Mom often talked about missing her other daughters, especially Christine. She had not seen her oldest daughter since she was a little girl. Christine, understandably, had abandonment issues and had voiced her desire never to see our mother again, but it was worth a try.

As soon as Christine answered, I told her what happened and begged her to help. "Please talk to Mom. Ask her to go to the hospital."

After some persuasion, Christine agreed. "Put her on the phone."

I overheard the conversation.

"This is Christine."

"Christine?" Mom whined.

"Please go to the hospital. If you do, I will come and visit you."

Mom exhibited no emotion. After several minutes of back and forth, she agreed.

"Please get in the ambulance when it arrives," Christine stressed.

"I will."

Relieved, I redialed 911. Mom was rushed to the hospital quickly after paramedics arrived. Daddy came and picked up the girls from my neighbor, allowing me to be with Mom.

Screaming and cursing greeted me as I walked into the emergency room. It was Mom—no surprise. Embarrassed, I sat in the waiting room until her exam was finished. The doctor explained there was no movement from her waist down.

"Her intense pain is caused from a grapefruit-sized abscess growing on her back."

"I—I don't understand." It was difficult to comprehend what I'd heard.

"We can't get her pain under control," the doctor explained. "She's been given enough pain-killers to take a rhino down."

My eyes widened.

"There's a high level of drugs in her system. Her use over the years makes her pain tolerance extremely low."

"What can be done?"

"I'd like to send her to UC Davis to remove the abscess on her back and try to control her pain."

Mom stayed in the hospital for two months, close to where Christine lived. Christine kept her word and visited her once a week. When she was released, a different woman came home.

Mom had lost much of her mobility. Her spine needed to be fused after the abscess was removed. Instead of five foot seven, she now stooped over at four foot ten.

Mom couldn't turn tricks anymore. Somehow, she still found someone to supply her with drugs, the only thing that eased her pain.

My life was out of control, and so was my bitterness and anger toward everyone, especially Mom. I blamed her for everything wrong in my life. Every time I thought about her, my body tensed. She was a disgrace of a mother. I hated her for what she'd done to me. Nevertheless, I moved in with her, so that she wouldn't be alone. It did help me with expenses.

I tried to keep my emotional distance, but my resentment showed. I did little to help besides cooking the meals. Mom was on her own, except that five-year-old Kiara helped as best she could. I cursed at her, called her disrespectful names, but mostly ignored her, just like she had ignored me. Sometimes I felt sorry for her. For the record, I'm not proud of the way I treated my mother.

It's also true that *my* mothering skills left a lot to be desired. I couldn't help myself. I was mad about who my mother was. Deep down inside, I knew I was no better. I didn't know how to change that. I just knew how to survive.

Since we lived together, Mom could watch my kids, so I went back to doing what I knew best. I re-activated my little black book, called my regulars, and continued to do drugs. I ignored my mother as well as my girls. My son lived with Daddy. My aggressive behavior went beyond my home. After a few months, I earned us another eviction. Fortunately, I found a nice big house to rent. Daddy allowed Andrew to go with us.

CHAPTER TWENTY-TWO

Roger lived down the street from our new house. He was a big guy, cute, but for me, he was just someone with whom to have a little fun. When Roger became obsessed with me, I wanted to break our relationship off, but it wouldn't be easy.

"I'm not going to be your girlfriend. I don't do boyfriends." After a brief back and forth, he became enraged. His eyes pierced mine, but I stood my ground.

"You cannot break up with me. I love you." Roger lunged toward me, put his hands on my waist, lifted me up, and threw me against the bathroom wall. "I love you too much to let you go."

After a few minutes, in excruciating pain, I picked myself up off the floor. Roger left that day but continued to call and come over. He begged me to be his friend. I finally relented. It just seemed easier.

But it wasn't over.

♦ ♦ ♦

"If I can't have you, no one will," Roger yelled at me a few days later.

"Go in the house, Andrew." I hated that my seven-year-old son was witnessing this. He did as he was told but stood peering through the screen door.

Roger grabbed my arm and pushed me off the raised front porch. He jumped on me with the full weight of his body. Fearing for my life, I rose up, but he pushed me back down. He stomped his foot into my stomach, again and again, leaving me defenseless. After he punched me in the face, blood began to seep from my mouth. Folding myself in the fetal position, I tried as best I could to protect myself. My only goal—to stay alive.

"Help me. Someone, please help me!" I yelled, hoping to be heard.

"Leave my mom alone!" Andrew cried. He ran out of the house, right up to Roger, and slapped him on his back. Roger brushed him off as if he were a piece of lint. Sirens screamed close by. The police were quickly at my side. They had been patrolling in the neighborhood when Mom called 911.

I sensed the presence of the officer who stood behind me. His gun was drawn. "Get down," the officer ordered Roger.

Roger backed off, putting his hands up. Remorse showed on his face. "I'm so sorry. I'm so sorry," he whined.

Dazed, I slowly sat up. With the officer's gun in his right hand pointed at Roger, the officer extended his left hand to me and pulled me to my feet. A rush of relief came over me. "Are you okay? You want me to call an ambulance?" he asked.

"No, I'll be okay." I couldn't let the officer see inside my house. I couldn't let him find the drugs. What would he say if he saw my severely malnourished and dirty kids? I couldn't let my kids go to Child Protective Services (CPS). And even though my body throbbed, I didn't think anything was broken.

"I don't need to go to the hospital. I'm fine."

"If you let Roger back in your house, we *will* call CPS." The officer nodded toward Andrew, who wouldn't leave my side. The girls stayed inside with Mom, out of sight.

Roger was arrested for assault and battery and spent the next month in jail, far away from us.

CHAPTER TWENTY-THREE

"Your grandma died."

I heard my aunt say the words, but it didn't seem real. Grandma's dead? Feeling lightheaded and sick to my stomach, I fell to my knees. "No. Grandma can't be dead."

"Her Bible lay open in her lap when she passed away." My aunt's words didn't quite register. How could my grandma die? Grandma was the one woman I could depend on to love me unconditionally. How could this wise, God-fearing woman be gone? How could she leave me?

My guilt wouldn't allow me peace where Grandma was concerned. She'd left this earth with the burden of my shame and disappointment on her mind. I wish I knew what passage she was reading when she died, but my aunt had closed her Bible when she found her.

Was she praying for me? I'll never know. The only times I'd called her the last few years of her life were when I needed something.

I'm so selfish.

I wanted to do better. I wanted Grandma to be proud of me.

Roger had returned into my life after he was released from jail. Why I let him come back, I don't know. The night before Grandma's funeral, we had a violent physical fight. He beat me badly. Unable to fully protect myself, I ended up with a large black eye, bruised lip, and a sore body. Roger ended up back in jail for assault and battery.

The next morning, when Daddy saw me, he was aghast. "You can't go to Grandma's funeral. People can't see you like that. Your presence would take away from her service."

Breaking out in sobs, I covered my face with my hands. I couldn't disagree with him. I drove to the cemetery but remained out of view until everyone left. Daddy waited for me.

I walked slowly over to the grave and knelt by her casket.

"Oh, Grandma. I love you so much. I know I've disappointed you. I'm so sorry. So sorry. I'm gonna miss you." My heart ached, and I gave way to uncontrolled sobs. As she was lowered into the ground, I watched and threw the first clumps of dirt on her casket.

"Grandma," I whispered. "I'm going to do better. I promise."

I sensed her whisper back, *I know*.

CHAPTER TWENTY-FOUR

The dream was vivid. A shadowy figure stood over me with a long-bladed knife, breathing hard. After I shook myself awake, terror gripped me.

This nightmare was real.

A glance at the clock told me it was two a.m. Where were my children?

"God help me!" I cried.

"You put me in jail," the man said, through clenched teeth. "You're going to pay."

I couldn't see his face, but I knew the voice. "Roger?"

He ripped the covers back as I jumped out of bed. With no time to stop him, he stomped over to Kendra's crib and shook her out of her sleep. I watched in horror as Roger held my precious daughter in one hand and a long-bladed hunting knife in the other.

"I'm going to slit her throat and then kill you." He swung her back and forth by the arms. Kendra began to whimper before breaking into a loud wail. My mothering instincts kicked in. I grabbed the knife on my nightstand as Roger turned his back and lunged toward him.

That's when my memory goes dark.

The next thing I recall, I was standing in my backyard, wondering how I got there. Rolling police lights lit the night sky. I later learned a neighbor watched as Roger tried to enter my house through a window and called the police.

An officer approached me. "What happened?"

They're going to take my kids. "Nothing."

My heart raced so fast I could hear it. I was dizzy and afraid. I couldn't think straight. How had I ended up talking to this officer? I couldn't remember.

"I need you to tell me what happened." The officer shined his flashlight on me but avoided my eyes. "One more time. What happened?"

"Nothing."

After the officer turned his flashlight on Roger, I gasped. Blood ran down his back.

"What happened to him?"

"You stabbed him." The officer peered directly at me. "Did he come into your house uninvited."

"I stabbed him? I don't remember."

"Something's going on here. I don't want to arrest you, but it may be the only way to get you out."

I kept quiet. What did he mean by that?

The officer handcuffed me, read me my rights, and put me in the back of the police car for a ride to the county jail. I was booked for assault with a deadly weapon with intent to cause serious injury or death. Apparently, Roger told the police he was in retreat when I attacked him, and he just tried to defend himself. How could I have ended up in a police car and not remember how I got there? How could I not know?

As usual, my hero—Daddy—picked up my kids and took them home

When my court-appointed attorney visited me after a few weeks in jail, I told him, to the best of my recollection, what had occurred.

"Roger said he was backing away when you attacked him with the knife."

"I don't remember stabbing him. I remember I was terrified he was gonna kill my baby."

My attorney opened the folder on the table and pulled out a few pictures. They were pictures of me with a badly bruised face, the result of Roger's attack on me the month before. I stared at them while he continued. "If you plead not guilty, you probably won't go home today. If you plead guilty, I may be able to get you released right away."

All I could think of was going home to my children. I had already spent three weeks in jail, and that was enough for me. I pled guilty to felony domestic violence. The judge gave me five years' probation plus one year of domestic violence intervention classes. I could go home and be with my babies. That was all that mattered.

CHAPTER TWENTY-FIVE

A year after Grandma died, Mom and I were evicted for failing to pay rent, which was an all too common story by now. I gave her all the money I had. She agreed to rent a big trailer, then come right back to get the kids and me. All the possessions I owned in the world sat on the front lawn, and everything had to be removed by five o'clock. My four children and I walked to the park across the street and waited. And waited. And waited. By three o'clock it was clear Mom wasn't coming back, and we had no place to go.

I called Daddy. When he pulled up in his pickup, the look on his face told me to be careful. When he jumped out of his vehicle, he used words that cannot be repeated. I wasn't sure if his anger was directed toward Mom or me or both. Daddy threw all our things into the back of his truck and drove the kids and me to his home.

My hero always came through when I needed him most—even when he was mad.

Single again, my dad now lived with one of my uncles in a nice home in the country. An empty trailer sat out back where Daddy put some of our things. He stored the rest in a shed. "You and the kids can stay in the trailer."

"Thank you, Daddy. I'm grateful to have a bed for my children." At least we didn't have to sleep in the park.

The next morning at breakfast, my uncle approached me. "Debra, do you want something different? Do you want to provide for your family?"

"Yes."

"You and the girls can have my master bedroom, and I'll take the couch. Andrew can stay with your Dad in the trailer." Putting his coffee cup down, he continued, "You don't need to give me money or pay rent but promise you will work to put your life back together."

"I will. I promise." This time I really meant it.

For the next year, we lived with my uncle, trying to make a fresh start. Meaning to begin a new life, I checked into school programs and found one for a dental technician. A fourteen-month class was perfect to start a real career and a new life.

My grades were excellent, but I didn't make friends or connect with "normal" people. Everywhere I walked, I imagined a big red scarlet letter lay plastered on my forehead for everyone to see. I kept a low profile, avoiding eyes and conversations with fellow students. I imagined nobody wanted to be my friend anyway, so why try?

♦ ♦ ♦

In the last phase of classes, a former client called. "Debbie, this is Rodney."

"Hi, Rodney. How are you?" I held my phone to my ear, already knowing what he wanted.

"You available for some fun?"

"Maybe." Making a little money to help get through school would be great. I could give it up after graduation.

But the pain I felt proved unbearable. The guilt and shame of what I was doing to myself, my kids, and my family kept me up at night. Then a friend offered the one thing that would take all my negative feelings away—meth. All my guilt and shame disappeared as soon as I took my first hit.

Before long, I quit school.

♦ ♦ ♦

Daddy blamed himself for how my life had spiraled out of control when I was a teenager. "If I had not sent you to live with your mother, this may never have happened. I'm so sorry, Debbie," he once told me.

Maybe that's why he always came to my rescue, but I saw how tired he was and the hurt on his face. It was my fault.

Daddy soon bought a house of his own with a trailer home out back. Since she seemed to have sobered up, Daddy agreed to let Mom move into the house with the kids and me, and he lived in the trailer. Her check helped pay Daddy rent and provided me with a built-in babysitter, leaving me free to run amuck. I began to take increasingly more advantage of Mom.

I reverted to my black book and made appointments for my time and favors. Most of my dates came from my list, but sometimes I enticed men off the streets. I followed men in my car and tempted them to pull over into a parking lot. Most of the time they were interested in what I had to offer.

It occurred to me I could make more money by recruiting girls to work for me. I drove them out to the streets just like Thomas had once driven me. I stayed in my car drinking coffee and watching, just like Thomas. The difference? I only took a portion of their profits.

After returning to Fresno, I walked into a hotel room to buy drugs. Sitting on the bed was Charlie, Darnell's son.

"Girl, where have you been," Charlie asked.

"Around. How's Darnell?"

"He passed away just after you left."

"Wow! I'm so sorry to hear that. Your dad was always good to me."

"What are you doing now, Little Debbie?"

"I'm on the streets working for myself."

"You need protection," Charlie said. "You took care of my dad, and I'll take care of you," he promised.

I knew he was right. I was a woman, so I needed protection. Charlie and I talked more, and he volunteered to protect me by making the other pimps think I was working for him. I was protected and free to do what I needed to do without fear. His girlfriend, Jenny, and I became fast friends. He took care of both of us.

Charlie watched out for me, and so did Nelson until he suffered a massive stroke. I felt some smidgen of gratitude that my kids had a home, however dysfunctional, and that they did not see what was going on. At least I hoped not.

How much worse could it get? My life was out of control, but I must have been the only one who didn't know it. I couldn't bring myself to admit how low my life had gotten.

An uneasiness came over me as I stepped into the home of one of my long-time drug suppliers, Sparks. Sitting alone in the smoke-filled living room, he nodded his head, motioning me toward the back room. I completed the transaction with the seller in the back, tucked my purchase in my backpack, and turned to leave.

Pop, pop, pop. The sound of gunshots rang loudly from the front of the house, hurting my ears. Startled, I feared I would be next. The seller pulled out his gun and headed toward the living room. I stayed back, in fear for my life.

Someone yelled, "They're gone. They shot him. Get out of here."

The pungent metallic smell of gunpowder filled the air as I rushed through the room where the shots had been fired. The lifeless body of the man, who had just minutes before been full of life, now lay slumped in a pool of blood. A lump formed in my throat, suffocating me. My heart raced faster than I could move. If they found me, the cops would arrest me. I had to get away.

My friend was waiting for me in the car across the street. He had witnessed two guys go into the house, heard the gunshots, and lowered his head. We were both terrified and knew how close we'd come to losing our lives.

"We could have died," I kept repeating. "We could have died. What would happen to my children if I'd been killed?" But I hadn't died. At least, not this time.

One night a few weeks later, I planned to visit Chris, a drug dealer I often partied with. But at the last minute, I decided to stay home with my kids. I was exhausted anyway. We were watching television when the phone rang. It was a friend.

"Chris was shot in the head. A gang member broke into his house tonight."

"Is he still alive?"

"Yes, but it doesn't look good."

My heart raced, and a chill zipped through me. I was supposed to be at that party. I could have been shot. Even then I realized it was by the grace of God that I had stayed home.

Within an hour of the first phone call, the phone rang again. "Chris didn't make it."

Was I next?

Still reeling over the shootings, too close for comfort, I told my friend, Jenny, "I'm going to be out of this business by Christmas."

And somehow, I knew I would.

CHAPTER TWENTY-SIX

Wednesday, December 24, 2008
My world was dark and sinister, and drugs ruled my life. My lifestyle was quickly losing its appeal. I was tired—just plain tired. Tired of running. Tired of my lifestyle. Sick and tired of being sick and tired. At five foot two and ninety-two pounds, I looked like the malnourished, ill woman I was. Each morning, I dressed in several layers of pants and tops to try and make myself look healthier.

There had to be a better life, but I didn't see a way. The police were after me, and I was headed to prison for sure. I had ignored probation and failed to attend court-ordered domestic violence classes. It was bound to catch up with me. The numerous warrants out for my arrest made me nervous.

My children were as safe as they could be. Mother cared for my kids the best she could, under the watchful eye of Daddy. He still lived in the trailer behind his house. It was technically my home too, but it was too dangerous to go there—the police were watching. I usually went under the cover of darkness, in the middle of the night, kissing my children as they slept. Slipping out always brought tears to my eyes and guilt to my soul.

It was Christmas Eve. There were no presents under the tree for my children from their mommy. My purse held $500. Luckily, the local drug store stayed open all night for holiday shoppers. At three a.m. on Christmas morning, I decided to take a chance.

All my problems were forgotten as I pushed the cart down the rows of toys, excitement flooding my heart. I bought dolls for each of the girls and added something special—a board game for Kiara, a set of toy dishes for Juliana, and a cute stuffed bear for Kendra. I found a big toy truck, just like the one Daddy drove, for Andrew. I added a board game for him too. I picked out wrapping paper, gift bags, and ribbon to make the presents look pretty. For Mom, I chose a gift set that included perfume, powder, and shower gel. The moment I found the t-shirt that read, "Best Papa," I knew it was for Daddy.

As I wrapped the gifts in the chill of the car, I hoped my kids would like them. When I finished, I drove to the house and sat for several hours, staring. Sadness overcame me as I remembered Christmases without my mommy. Now my kids were forced to face the holidays without theirs. How could I keep doing this?

♦ ♦ ♦

Christmas Morning
December 25, 2008

Early in the morning, I finally pulled myself together, dried my eyes, got out of my car with my treasures in hand, and walked toward the porch. Hoping the police would take a holiday, I gained the courage I needed to go through the door. The sights, sounds, and smells of Christmas met me. Daddy had done his best to make the day memorable for the kids.

"Mommy! Mommy!" The children yelled at once when they saw me walk into the house. I put down the gifts to greet each one, hugging them. Tears welled in my eyes and the kids' as well. Their hugs felt so warm and welcoming.

"I have presents for you." I cheerfully handed them out.

They opened their gifts quietly and each said, "Thank you, Mommy." My heart sank as I sensed no joy or excitement. They were only interested in hanging out with me. With all four of my children surrounding me, we hugged, kissed, and talked. Their full attention focused on their mother. Nothing else mattered. Nothing else except the threat of the police knocking on the door.

I didn't dare stay too long. After an hour, I told my disappointed children that I had to go.

"Don't go, Mommy," four-year-old Kendra cried. Her body shook, and she sobbed, her heart visibly breaking. "Don't go, Mommy. Don't go, Mommy."

"I have to, sweetheart." I pulled away, tears streaming down my face. "Mommy doesn't want to, but I have to." Soon, all the kids were crying and asking me to stay. Watching my children become so upset, was almost more than my heart could take. Lord, help me! If I didn't go soon, the police were going to show up.

I broke myself away, bawling as hard as they were. I ran to the car, got in, and drove a few blocks. I pulled over and parked. Laying my head against the steering wheel, I broke down, heaving with sobs. "God, I don't want to go to prison. I love my kids. I don't know what to do. Help me. I don't deserve it, but please help me!"

After getting myself together, I picked up my friend. There were no Christmas presents or Christmas dinner for us. We spent the rest of the day picking up whatever dates we could. Most of our regulars were home with their families, where

I longed to be. The last of my money spent on my kids, I was left broke, and I needed to earn more to support my drug habit.

It turned dark at 5:30 p.m. on Christmas night. My friend and I decided to grab a bite to eat at the one fast food place we knew was open but decided to get fuel first. I pulled into a gas station.

Why did I pull in here, right in full view of the police?

I'd hidden all day, but now it was over. The officer made eye contact with me.

Do I know him?

Officer Cuyler, a giant of a man, stepped out of his vehicle and walked straight toward me. I hesitated before putting my car in drive. Officer Cuyler opened my door and reached inside to turn the ignition off.

"I finally got you!" he triumphantly exclaimed. "Get out." Officer Cuyler's stern voice broke my will. I did as he said. There was nothing I could do. I had run long enough.

After reading my rights, he gently guided me into the back seat of the patrol car. Before he closed the door, he said, "*Allah yusallmak!*"

"What?" I stared at him, puzzled.

"*May God protect you*, in Arabic." He closed the door.

A strange sense of serenity spread over me as Officer Cuyler pulled the parole cruiser onto the freeway and headed toward the county jail. I was surprised when the heavy burdens of my world suddenly lifted. It was a relief to be caught, like a bird flying free.

Over my short lifetime, I was arrested many times, but that night, something felt different—*very* different.

CHAPTER TWENTY-SEVEN

Christmas Night 2008

The holding cell was usually packed to the max with standing room only. Strangely, that night—Christmas night—it stood empty. I was all alone, and I picked up the phone to call my daddy, who would come to my rescue. He always did.

"Daddy, I've been arrested."

He didn't say anything but listened until I finished. "Debbie, I love you so much, but I cannot do this anymore. I'm going to tell you this only one time. The kids will always be okay. I will take care of them. I'm not coming to see you. I'm not putting money on the books. You're going to have to figure this out on your own. Don't call the house. Don't call me." Without giving me a chance to respond, my daddy, my hero, the man who I could always count on, hung up.

I must not have heard right. My daddy wouldn't abandon me. I dialed his number back... No answer. I tried several times. There must be something wrong with the phone. My daddy would not do this.

"Officer, this phone isn't working."

"It's working."

My Mom needed to know where I was and what Daddy had said. I called a good customer and asked him to call my mother.

After I hung up the phone, the full realization that my Daddy had rejected me hit me like an arrow to the heart. Clutching my chest, I let myself fall to the floor, pulling my knees to my chin. I suddenly felt so embarrassed of the ugly person staring back at me, reflected on the bars of the cell—ashamed that my kids knew me this way. What had I become?

I felt something somewhere from deep within—a cry from my heart—a place of profound aloneness. I sat alone for three and a half hours pouring out my soul to the one-person Grandma taught me would listen—God.

After rejecting Him for so many years, would He still be willing to listen? Would He care? No person in this world wanted me. God must hate me too. I'm a terrible mother. How could God, in any way, look down from His mighty throne and see the wretched person I had become and want to do anything for me? How could He care about someone like me?

There was no other choice. I had to try.

In my spirit, I cried out. *Lord, Lord, please just look at me.* Over and over I heard the cry inside of me. For the first time in my life, I knew I wasn't going to fix this. There was only one who could—God.

God, I prayed, *if there is any possibility, you're still listening to me, please take me back. Take care of my children. Please, God, let me see them again.*

The same powerful presence that overtook me at camp when I was twelve years old occupied the room. A wave of emotion flooded my mind. Uncontrolled tears surged forth. I sat in that cell alone, crying, praying, pleading with God. When I was abducted, it wasn't my fault. But the decisions made over the last eight years were entirely my own doing. "I did that," I confessed out loud. "God, whatever you want to do to me, I deserve. Just let me talk to my kids." After praying, I sensed that everything was going to be all right and fell into a deep, peaceful sleep.

I knew Daddy meant what he said. He wasn't going to come and see me, and I wasn't going to talk to my kids. But when I woke up on December 26, the day after Christmas, I felt this overwhelming urge to call home. The night before, I could not get through because Daddy had blocked the phone. But something told me to redial the number. I had nothing to lose. To my surprise, the call went through. Mom answered and accepted the call.

"Hi, baby, how are you?" Mom sounded concerned.

A breath of relief escaped my lips. "*Whew.* Whoever took the block off the phone, thank you."

"No one took the block off the phone. You'd better not tell your dad I took this call," Mom warned.

"Let me talk to the kids," I begged. Mom put them on the phone. I savored every minute of the words spoken between us, even though they all cried. I called home several times the next week. Each time I managed to get through. Each time Mom took my collect call.

A week later, I asked my son, "Put Papa on the phone."

"Hello."

"This is Debbie."

"How are you calling me?"

"Dad, you don't need to talk to me, but let me talk to my children." He said he wouldn't take the block off the phone, but he allowed me to talk to the kids that day.

Still, I continued to call home, miraculously without a problem, until three weeks before I was released from jail. Dad never received a bill for those calls.

Usually a person would go before the judge within seventy-two hours of being arrested. Weekends and holidays didn't count. Since Christmas was on a Thursday, it was five days before I appeared in court.

For the first time, no one came to support me. My dad was not there. It was just me, my court-appointed attorney, and God. I was tired. It had been five days, and the drugs were leaving my system. I didn't care.

Judge, tell me what I already know—that I'm going to prison for the next four or five years. I just want this over. I'm exhausted.

The judge asked, "How do you plea?"

"No contest."

The judge paused for a minute and looked me directly in the eyes. "Ms. Woods, I don't know why, but I'm going to give you a second chance. I am giving you 180 days, minus time served. But if I ever see you in this courtroom again, you're going to prison. Do you understand?"

"Yes, sir. Thank you."

The judge pounded his gavel. "Next case!"

I turned to my court-appointed attorney. "What happened?"

"The court has credited you with time served. Eighty-six days."

Later in the day, I called Mother. "Mom, can you put the kids around the phone? I just want to pray with all of you, if that's okay."

After the kids got on the phone, with Mom listening in, I said, "I love all of you and miss you so much. I need for you to be strong and good for Nana." Pausing to clear the lump lodged in my windpipe, I continued, "Let me pray over you."

I could hear the sniffles on the other end of the phone, but I knew I had to leave my kids something to hang on to. A prayer was the only thing I had to give. "God, protect my precious children. Help them to be strong and courageous while I'm gone. Watch over them and me. Keep us safe until we are all together again. Amen."

My heart lay shattered in a thousand pieces, but a peace flooded over me. "Mom, I love you so much. I need you more now than ever. I don't care about anything that has happened in the past. Right now, I need you to hold it together and take care of my kids. Please, Mom. I know I have said hurtful things over the years. I want you to know I'm sorry. It hasn't been easy living with me. I'm so sorry I've been so hateful and abusive. I hope you'll forgive me."

Mom stayed very quiet on the other end until I finished talking. When I'd finished, she spoke. "I love you, Debbie. Your little ones will be fine."

"Thank you, Mom." I stumbled over the words as emotion thickened my tongue. "I'll be home as soon as I can. Things will be different. I promise."

On the walk back to my cell, my body heaved with sorrow, weeping over my children and my relationship with my mom. Back in my cell, I fell on my bunk, desperate for all that had been lost.

CHAPTER TWENTY-EIGHT

"Debbie?"

I looked up at the sound of my name and found a familiar face looking back. "Terri! What are you doing here?"

Terri was well known on the streets as the bottom girl for a notorious pimp and drug dealer. A bottom girl is the most trusted of the pimp's girls and has usually been with her pimp the longest. She is the most loyal and prominent in value.

"Big bust with Spider last July. I'm a federal case," Terri explained. "What are you in for?"

"Not following through on probation and stuff like that. I'll be out in a few months."

"Lucky you."

"I heard about that big bust last year. I didn't know you'd been arrested." Terri was part of a gang, well known by the police for drug trafficking, assaults with deadly weapons, murder, the exploitation of women and girls, and other illegal activities.

"I kept trying to call you last year. How come you never called me back?"

I shrugged. "I meant to, but a friend found out I was going to call you, so he grabbed my phone and smashed it. Said he didn't want me near another pimp, especially the man you were with."

"Let me show you something." Terri opened her case file and pointed to a page. "Look. Your name is here." The transcript of the recorded conversation during which I promised to call her back lay in front of me. My breath caught. It occurred to me that if I'd gone to meet her, I could have been caught up and arrested with her and her pimp. Several times I had planned to meet with Terri, and each time something stopped me. Once my car wouldn't start. Had God protected me? I began to revisit all the serendipities over the years and realized, for the first time, that maybe He had.

Terri and I became good friends in jail and ended up sharing a cell. I knew Terri was headed to prison. I could have been going with her, but I wasn't. Thank you, God.

In jail, I attended every chapel and Bible study available, even the Spanish services. It didn't matter that I couldn't understand the words, I understood the heart. With my childhood background in church, I knew who God was. I'd accepted him as my personal Savior when I was a teenager at summer camp.

Unbeknownst to me, I soon became known as a religious leader, like I had been the last time I was in jail. I had no problem telling the other women about Jesus. I freely told others about Him and started a Bible study with several girls desperate for a word of hope. One inmate, Cindy, didn't have friends, and she never received money from anyone. Her skin had scaly spots on it, so no one wanted to be around her. I was lucky. Mother received a public assistance check every month to take care of my children. She made sure I had money, at least twenty dollars, on my books. Daddy showed tough love, kept his promise, and provided me with nothing. The money I got from Mother was used to buy items from the jail store, or commissary, as it was called. I would share with Cindy, giving her some coffee or a bag of chips whenever I could.

"I have a big bag of stuff coming," Cindy said. "When it comes, I'm gonna give you a few things to repay you."

"You don't have to do that."

"No, I want to."

I didn't believe Cindy had anything coming, but a few days later a large box arrived for her. Once she got it, she headed straight for her cell, bypassing me entirely. At the time, I was in the company of some heavy hitters or jail leaders—those whom others feared. When they saw Cindy snub me, they started in.

"That girl is treating you like a fool," one quipped.

"You shouldn't have given her nothing," said another.

"She tricked you."

"You got played."

I began to think that; indeed, Cindy had disrespected me. It annoyed me that she was making me look bad in front of the others. One didn't want to look weak to the other inmates, or they would take advantage of you by beating you up or casting you out of the group. There was only one thing I could do.

I purposely walked up to Cindy, my hands on my hips. "Hey, did you forget about me?"

Cindy ignored me. I rushed into her cell and grabbed the stuff out of her box. But in my heart, I was torn. This was precisely the kind of thing I was always speaking to the women about. I talk about God, and then I do *this*?

Terri walked in and stared at me. "I knew you were a fake. You sit here and talk all this Jesus stuff. You do all these Bible studies, then you run in here and take this girl's stuff?"

Remorseful, I threw the things I had snatched from Cindy in the air and ran to my cell. I grabbed my Bible and started to cry. I was angry and sick to my stomach. I had made an epic failure. Terri and her friends were going to beat me up because I didn't attack Cindy. I would be viewed as weak. Eat or be eaten. I was going to be eaten. What was I going to do?

I held up my Bible and sobbed. "God, You promised me. You promised me that You would not let any temptation overtake me. You promised me You would always provide a way of escape." The others must have thought I was crazy as they listened to me.

"Woods, roll up." I heard the command over the loudspeaker, just like eight years earlier. My whole body went cold.

Terri snickered, assuming I was being called because of the scene I'd just caused in Cindy's cell. "They just called you to roll up."

Were they coming to take me to isolation?

I got my things together and waited for them to take me to lockdown. The resentfulness showed in my body language and my tone of voice.

The guard shifted her feet. "You ready?"

"Whatever." I gave her a sneer.

"If you don't want to go to the work pod, let me know, and I'll take you back." In the work pod, you get to work and have four visits a week instead of two. It's a step up.

My eyebrows shot into my forehead. "I'm going to the work pod?"

"Unless you don't want to."

It saddened me that Terri saw me act in such a disrespectful way, but I couldn't deny I was glad to be out of there. I had messed up, really messed up bad. Lesson learned.

With my new freedom in the work pod, I rose at four each morning and was given my sack breakfast and lunch. I returned to my cell to eat and spend time with Jesus before my day started. After less than two weeks in the work pod, I tried to make a call home, but the phone was blocked. There was no one I could call. It had been three weeks since Mom had come to visit. My mind filled with all the reasons why—none of them logical reasons. At the time, they all felt real.

Church and reading my Bible continued to be important. Walking into my new chapel service, my heart leaped when I saw Sharon Hoard. Sharon had been my school nurse and counselor when I was in grammar school. She helped me through some tough times when I was growing up. And now she was teaching in our chapel. Disregarding the rules, I grabbed her in a hug.

"Are you still at the Easton school?" I asked her

"I am."

"Have you seen my kids?"

"Yes, I saw them yesterday."

The chapel service was starting, but when she was done, Sharon stayed back with me to talk.

"Will you visit my family and let them know I can't contact them."

"I absolutely will," Sharon assured me with a wink.

Mom visited me the next day and said Sharon had come to see her. She explained that the car hadn't been working. The next time Sharon came to give chapel, she told me that she had called all four of my kids into her office to tell them she had seen me and that I was all right. She told them their mommy loved them.

And the hole in my heart got bigger. The hole only my kids could fill.

On March 20, 2009, at midnight, I was released. I asked Mom to bring my kids, even though it would be late. When I stepped out into the waiting room at exactly 12:10 a.m., screams of joy greeted me as my kids, all at once, jumped to hug me. As my heart filled with the sweet love of my children, I took in every moment.

"Mommy," five-year-old Kendra said, handing me red rosary beads.

"What's this sweetheart?"

"The old man in the corner asked me if I was here to see my mommy. He gave me this and told me to give it to you."

"Where is he? I want to thank him."

"Over there." Kendra said. I looked in the direction she indicated. The corner was empty. "Oh, he's gone."

A few weeks after being released from jail, I heard a soft knock on our door. I peeked out from the curtain covering the front door window. Mrs. Hoard, the woman who visited the chapel at the jail to teach, stood on my porch.

Puzzled, I opened the door. "Hi, Mrs. Hoard."

"D—Debra, would you like to have a Bible study with me?"

I couldn't believe what I'd heard. This amazing Christian woman wanted to spend time with me? "Yes, Mrs. Hoard! I'd love to have a Bible study with you!" I answered quickly before she could change her mind.

SHARON HOARD

CHAPTER TWENTY-NINE

Sharon's Story

While sitting in my regular church pew one Sunday, listening to the pastor deliver his message, my thoughts drifted to the Bible study I planned to teach later that afternoon with ladies in the county jail. My ministry lay in my career as a school nurse and my volunteer work as a jail Bible teacher. A thought suddenly entered my mind: *You need to have a Bible study with Debra Woods.* I knew the message was from God because I would have never thought of that on my own. *Never.*

I can't do a Bible study with Debra Woods.

Yes, you can.

But God, I argued. *Debra and I have a tense relationship. I don't respect her. She's not a good mother. Her kids come to school dirty, and she doesn't take care of them. They don't even come to school much of the time. And besides, how am I supposed to work with someone who's a druggie? No, don't think so.*

You are to do a one-on-one Bible study with her.

God must have made a mistake, I thought. I'd never taught a one-on-one Bible study.

Growing up in a loving Christian home, my family regularly attended church. I never drank, smoked, or used drugs. As an educated, middle-class woman, there was nothing Debra and I had in common. Why would God want me to build a relationship with someone like her?

I walked out of the church knowing there was no way I would do a Bible study with Debra Woods. Going to the jail twice a month on Sunday was one thing, but this was asking for much more. There was no way I was going to get close to Debra Woods.

But a few hours later the thought came back.

Sharon, do a Bible study with Debra Woods. It was more of a command than a request.

"No, God!" I said out loud.

Lead her in a Bible study.

This battle continued into the night.

Call her, Sharon.

"No!"

Back and forth and back and forth, the battle went on. In the wee morning hours, exhausted, a fitful sleep finally came. The next day, the fight continued to rage within me. Realizing God wasn't going to give me any rest, I finally relented.

"Okay God, but I don't feel like it."

So, Monday afternoon, with a less-than-positive attitude, I picked up the phone and dialed the number I had on file for Debra, hoping she wouldn't answer.

"*This number has been disconnected. If you think you have reached this number in error hang up and dial again*," the recorded message said.

Relieved, I looked up and spoke to God. "See. I tried."

Not good enough. Try harder.

I knew I wasn't going to have any peace until I'd made every effort to get in touch with Debra. There was only one thing to do. Get in my car and drive the short distance from the school to her home.

When I arrived, there was no car in the driveway. *Good.*

Get out of the car and go to the door, God impressed upon me.

I knocked on the door in the absence of a doorbell, thinking—hoping—she wasn't home.

I saw Debra peek through the curtain on the door window. She opened the door. "Hi, Mrs. Hoard."

"D—Debra, would you like to have a Bible study with me?"

Without hesitation, Debra said, "Yes, Mrs. Hoard! I'd love to have a Bible study with you!"

I was stunned that she'd agreed so quickly and joyously. We decided on a time to meet the following week. Still, I was less than enthusiastic about what I had just committed to. My knees weakened as I walked back to my car. Once I'd closed the car door, a long sigh released from deep inside. What had I gotten myself into?

As the school nurse at Orange Center Elementary School, I knew the students who visited me regularly. Debra had been one of those students. She often complained of stomach aches and had a habit of twisting her long hair, breaking it off.

"Why do you twist your hair, Debra?" I once asked her.

"Uh," she answered. "I think about my mom a lot. I wish she weren't in prison. I wish she was home with me, like everyone else's mother. I miss her."

When Debra's mom wasn't in prison, Debra worried about her because she used drugs. This all affected Debra's grades and behavior. She was a smart, cute, petite girl, but her feistiness and foul mouth often got her into trouble with the teachers. I knew Debra was hurting more than she let on.

Once she graduated out of grade school, I forgot all about her.

Years later, my path crossed with Debra's again when I walked through the door of a jail classroom and a skinny young lady walked up to me and exclaimed, "Mrs. Hoard!"

My mouth dropped. I knew who she was instantly. "Debra. Hello."

I knew her children very well. I worried about them. I knew that their grandmother, who watched after them whenever Debra wasn't around, was an alcoholic. They often missed school, looked malnourished and dirty, and were frequently sent home with head lice. Other kids made fun of them.

After our Bible study at the jail ended, Debra came up to me and pleaded with me to check on her kids.

"I'll be happy to do that for you." I touched her arm. The rules did not allow me to hug her, though Debra had broken that rule when she first saw me. The next day, I called each one of Debra's children into my office, one by one. Each conversation went something like this: "I talked to your Mom. Do you know where she is?"

Each of them hung their heads in embarrassment. "Jail."

"Your mom loves you. She asked me to check on you." As I spoke, a shy smile crossed each face. "Can I pray with you. Would you like that?"

After they each nodded their heads, I held each of their hands. Together, we prayed for their mother and for them. My memories of those conversations are sweet but sad.

Now that I had a date scheduled for Bible study with Debra, I realized I didn't have a clue how I could help her. I ask God to give me guidance. "I'm relying on you," I told Him. I'd always had the comfort of going to the jail, teaching, then leaving. This one-on-one study would be much more involved.

On an early spring day, I drove to Debra's house to start our time together. Debra had rededicated her life to Christ while in jail, so for her first Bible study, I chose one for new Christians.

Debra walked out to the car to greet me before I could get out. "Hi, Mrs. Hoard."

"Good to see you, Debra." I embraced her. She didn't act or look like a Christian. I still wasn't sure how I could help her.

"Is it okay if we just sit outside?"

"Okay." I agreed, even though it was a bit warm out.

Debra motioned me to an old, dirty, dark-green plaid couch on the porch. A ragged, cream-colored blanket lay over the seat, making it a bit more inviting. I sat down first and found it to be more comfortable than it looked. There was an earthy animal smell in the air. Several dogs and cats played in the yard and would sometimes visit us as we sat. I looked at Debra. "Can I pray first?"

"Yes, please." She bowed her head, and I took her hand.

"Lord, thank you for this opportunity to spend time in the Word with Debra. Thank you in advance for what you are going to reveal and the work you are going to do in both of us. Amen." I gave her a workbook and a Bible, and we began what would prove to be a long, meaningful journey together.

Several weeks into the study, a car drove up while we sat outside studying. Two men were inside the car. Debra whispered, "You have to get out of here right now. Immediately."

"Why?"

"Right now, you have to leave!" she said, more forcefully.

She was serious.

I gathered my things and quickly walked to my car. I wondered if those guys were there to sell drugs. Was Debra still doing drugs? This wasn't going to work. *I'm not coming back.*

But then, something stirred in my heart. *Don't assume anything.*

And so, the next week, I came back. Week after week after week. Slowly, my heart toward Debra changed. I began to care about her, and that care grew into a special love for her. One thing became clear—Debra wanted to change, but she didn't know how to do it.

Early in September, I asked Debra, "Why don't you and your kids start going to church? I called the New Beginnings church close by and was told someone would pick you and the kids up."

"I'll think about it," she said.

But she never went.

A few weeks later, I got up the gumption to broach the subject again. "Why don't you go to church?"

She bit her lip and didn't reply for a few moments. Then she took a long, deep breath, tears brimming her eyes. "I just know that when I walk into that church, they'll be able to tell I'm not their kind."

I put my hand on her shoulder and looked her in the eye. "Just go once. I truly believe you and your kids will be accepted. Be brave and courageous. God will go with you, and I'm here to help you too."

"Okay."

The next Sunday, a crisp October day, Debra and her kids attended The New Beginnings Church.

At the church, a Fall festival was planned for Halloween. Debra felt more comfortable than she had imagined that first day, and she and her kids even volunteered to work a booth at the event. As our Bible studies continued, I became her mentor—almost like a mom. I felt the weightiness of the responsibility, as if I were indeed her parent.

Each day when Debra picked up her children from school, I would still be on campus. I noticed she wore low-cut tops and short shorts. A sexually explicit tattoo decorated her thigh, which shocked me and others on staff. I could tell her junior-high son was embarrassed and tried to stay a little distance from her. I brought her some modest clothes, and we discussed proper attire for a mother and a Christian. She listened and slowly changed her wardrobe.

Debra's home was just two houses from the school, making it easy for the teachers to learn I was mentoring Debra. The second-grade teacher approached me. "Would you please talk to Debra about her kids always coming to school so dirty?" I agreed I would and prayed for the right opportunity. On my next visit, a dirty, pink jacket lay on the porch floor. "Does your daughter wear this jacket to school?"

"Yes, she does. Why?"

"Do you see how dirty it is?" I held it up. Dirt and old food stains covered the front. "When teachers see this, they think you're not doing a good job as a mom."

"I can't help it. They get out of the house before I get up."

"Debra, it's our job as mothers to be up before our kids to make sure they are properly fed and clean before they go out the door. It's up to you to make sure your children get to school on time."

She nodded. "Okay, I'll try."

As the weather became chilly, I wondered how sitting outside was going to work. When I arrived for our meeting in mid-November, Debra didn't run out to meet me like she normally did. Something must have been wrong. I cautiously knocked on the door. After a minute, Debra answered.

"Come in, Mrs. Hoard." She cheerfully motioned me inside.

I stood stunned for a minute. Up until now, Debra hadn't seemed to want me to see the inside of her house. "I'd love to come in. It's a bit cold today."

Debra's house was a bit messy, but it looked like she'd made an effort to straighten up. I learned later that Debra had cleaned the house just for me. Over time, her home became immaculate, as well as other areas of her life.

A year after we started meeting, I was sitting in the teachers' lounge when the same teacher who had encouraged me to talk to Debra said, "Sharon, you are doing miracles with the Woods kids."

"What do you mean?"

"They are coming to school clean, fed, and their grades are soaring."

Another teacher added, "You *are* doing a great job of changing Debra and the kids."

"It is absolutely not me. Only God can change anyone. I am just the vehicle," I replied firmly.

The teachers didn't agree and kept praising me, but I knew the truth. It was God. Debra's progress was slow but steady. Gradually, she was maturing into a beautiful, loving lady and mother, right before my eyes.

Two years after we began meeting together, I admitted to Debra, "I don't think I was the best one to mentor you because I've never gone through what you have."

She stared at me with her wide brown eyes. "Oh, no. For a woman like me to be friends with a church woman like you means more than you'll ever know. For you to accept me and love me means so much."

And I did. I had come to love Debra and her kids. During that time, we spent a lot of time doing fun things together—celebrating birthdays, going to dinner, the movies, the zoo, and many other adventures. Still, Debra's past followed her. It took a year and a half for her to land her first job. She eventually got a better one and then an even better one. As she started working more, our time together dwindled.

After she returned from a women's retreat, she attended in Pinecrest, she called me. "Sharon, I want to start an organization to help rescue women who are on the street like I was."

"That's a wonderful dream," I said.

But I secretly doubted she would be able to do it.

CHAPTER THIRTY

Debra

Mom managed to keep it together and take care of my kids while I sat in jail. For that I was grateful. Once I came home though, she started her old addictions, spiraling out of control. Something wasn't quite right with her. I sensed evil spirits when she was around. My pastor, along with church members, agreed to bless my home. They walked through the house and prayed over the beds, couches, doorways, and windows for over an hour. I hung a cross over the door. All our activity disturbed Mom.

"I can't have this!" she screamed, visibly shaken. She hobbled outside using her cane. Mom still couldn't stand up straight because of her fused spine.

That night, she refused to come inside the house. She acted like a deranged woman. Night after night she slept in my car or on the couch outside. She refused to take baths and squatted under a tree to relieve herself. No matter how much I coaxed, she wouldn't budge.

"Mom, please come into the house."

"I can't breathe in there. I'm just fine out here."

"Will you at least go to church with me?"

She reluctantly agreed but didn't want to go inside the building. After more prodding, she stepped into the doorway, unbathed, smelling like an old garbage can full of spoiled food. I didn't care. I was just glad she was there.

But what happened next absolutely mortified me.

Mom usually wore an adult diaper due to her incontinence, but on this day she didn't. We were in church less than ten minutes when Mom said, "I guess I can't be in here anymore."

"Why?"

"I just peed on the pew." She got up and walked out.

I couldn't believe the wet, smelly mess my own mother made. *God help me. Help me have patience with Mom.* I wanted to scream. Instead, I remained calm.

"Come on kids, let's go." I left as quickly as I could and hoped no one would know it was a grown woman who'd messed the pew.

Mom eventually came back into the house, but I had to remove the cross from the door. She never set foot inside a church again.

During all those wasted years of hard living, my house was always a total, disorganized mess. My children were forced to live in filth. With the help of Sharon Hoard, that all changed. I worked on being a better mother and providing them with a healthy home. One day, I found syringes inside the toilet tank.

"Mom!" I yelled, remembering the many times I had hidden paraphernalia in the same place.

"What?"

"What is this? Why do you have these needles in here?"

"Not mine. Maybe they're yours."

"You know they aren't mine! I want you out of my house—*today*!"

Mom left and slammed the door behind her. She wasn't gone a minute when she walked back into the house and grabbed her suitcase, which she'd already packed. She had planned to leave all along. It wasn't soon enough. I continued to yell and curse at her, not caring that the neighbors heard us. I was glad my kids and Mrs. Hoard weren't there to witness the scene.

I didn't hear from Mom until the next Christmas. She'd just disappeared. With her gone, I noticed my children seemed to relax. I hadn't detected how tense they'd become until Mom was out of the picture. A calming presence settled over the house. It was nice.

A few days after Mom left, seven-year-old Juliana came into my room with something obviously on her young mind. "Mommy, I got to talk to you. I want to tell you something, but I don't want you to be mad. I don't want you to hurt or kill Nana."

Hurt or kill Nana? Juliana had my attention. I took her hands in mine and gazed into her eyes. "Talk to me, sweetheart. It's going to be okay."

"Eddie touched me."

My heart sank. I knew I had to get as much information out of her as I could. I controlled my emotions and encouraged her to tell me more.

"Nana took Kendra and me to a hotel where Eddie lived while she took Kiara to the hospital."

Anger began to rise from the pit of my stomach. My jaw tightened, but I kept calm, not wanting to scare Juliana. Eddie was a john, a friend of Mom's, and a former customer. She would call him if she needed something. He would call me if he wanted to buy sex. He'd often asked me to act like a child, so I believed him to be a pedophile and that he should be kept from children. Mother and I had talked about Eddie several times. I specifically told her never to allow the kids to be around him.

I knew of the time Mom took Kiara to the hospital. She had jumped off the bed and hurt her foot. When it hadn't gotten better after a few days, I'd asked Mom to take her to the hospital. Even then, I warned her, "Mom whatever you do, do not allow Eddie to care for the kids."

"I won't," Mom promised.

But here Juliana was telling me that Mom had broken her word. I'd trusted Mom, but I should have known better.

"What happened?"

"He told me to put Kendra in the shower. There were toys under the table he said I could play with." She paused, "He opened his pants and asked if I liked what I saw. Then he tried to put his hands in my panties. I cried and told him no. Then Grandma walked in."

Anger seethed beyond the surface of my emotions. How could my mother do this to her own granddaughter? Would it ever stop for her? *I will never forgive Mom for this. She can hurt me but not my kids.*

My heart ached for what my daughter had endured. Shame filled my heart for the life my children had been forced to live because I'd failed to be the mother they deserved.

After comforting Juliana, I called the police and filed a report. A police officer came to my door soon after to take my statement. All the usual questions were asked. "How did I find out? What happened? When did it happen? Where did it happen? But then the questioning took a turn. I wasn't prepared.

"What was your relationship to Eddie?"

I told the truth. He had once been a client.

The officer then started to ask me questions about my lifestyle.

"Do you understand that if you had made different choices in life, this wouldn't have happened?"

Frustrated, I asked him, "Why are you asking these questions? Are you saying that this is *my* fault? Are you saying my daughter deserves this because of *me*?"

The officer looked me in the eyes. "What I'm telling you is that there is no court that would convict him. We've spoken to Eddie, and he's telling us that you're mad because he refused to give you money, so how do I know you're not just disgruntled? It's your word against his."

I later found out that Eddie had offered to care for the girls while Mom took Kiara to the hospital. She initially said no, but a bribe of a case of beer changed her mind. Mom came back early from the hospital because the emergency room wasn't busy, allowing Kiara to get right in and out. Eddie wasn't expecting her back so soon.

Another miracle.

When the police confronted Mom, she told them she didn't have a choice. "I didn't know this would happen," she said.

Eddie needed to pay for the position he put my daughter in. I wanted Mom to pay too. But no one would help me. There wasn't enough proof. They couldn't go on the word of a child, and the adults denied it. I cried out to God. "You are a big God. You can take care of this. I don't want any more kids to get hurt because of that man. You know he isn't going to stop! Please don't let him hurt another child."

Three years later, I learned Eddie had died in his hotel room. He lay there several days before the motel manager found him.

"Thank you, Lord," I whispered.

As far as I was concerned, Mom needed to be in prison for selling my daughter and putting her in a dangerous situation. I sent a text message to her: "Stay gone." I didn't see her for several months after that.

What kind of person was my so-called mother? How could she sell her granddaughter? How could she have sold her daughter, for that matter?

I studied my Bible every day. But I still cursed, smoked, and dressed like my profession hadn't changed. And it still amazed me that Mrs. Hoard wanted to meet with me weekly to work through a Bible study. She encouraged me to take my kids to church, but I was afraid. I feared the upstanding Christian Church people only saw a red scarlet letter on my forehead.

With my mother out of the picture, my family rallied around me again. As I grew in God, and with the encouragement of Mrs. Hoard, I slowly became convicted to change the way I dressed and the way I talked. I knew things had changed for the better when an uncle said to me, "Debra, you are a pleasure to be around."

"Really?" I flashed a huge smile. "I like me a lot better too."

I wished Grandma could see me now.

CHAPTER THIRTY-ONE

I needed a job—a real job. I drove to a wrecking yard I knew needed help. The owner hired me two days later. Having a respectful job felt exciting. Before I'd worked my first full week, my uncle drove up in the yard. Something was terribly wrong.

"It's your dad." He told me my dad and Roxie, Dad's girlfriend, were riding his motorcycle when an SUV pulled out in front of them.

"Is he all right?"

"He's still alive but badly hurt."

My uncle sped us to the hospital, running at least one red light. Dad had significant head injuries, broken bones, and internal bleeding. The doctors didn't know if he would make it. If he did, he might not be the same.

I couldn't believe how broken and mangled Daddy appeared. He looked like he might die at any minute. *God, don't take my daddy. Let him see me completely healthy. Let Daddy know that I've made it,* I prayed. I deeply regretted that my grandma died while I was still on the streets. I didn't want that for my dad. He couldn't leave this earth not knowing that his little girl was going to be okay. I now knew for sure I would never go back to what I was.

Love for my dad overflowed as I sat with him, thinking of all he had sacrificed for me and his grandchildren. I held his hand and asked God to save him. I needed Daddy. My kids needed their grandpa.

"Daddy, I love you so much. You have always been there for me, even when I didn't deserve it." I choked. "I've promised before, but I mean it this time. I will make my life better. You will be proud of me—cross my heart. I promise, Daddy." He didn't respond, but I hoped he could hear me.

I kissed his hand. "Daddy, you are my hero. You're the best gift God ever gave me. I love you." I broke down sobbing, willing Daddy to live. I spent hours by his side making promises I knew I would keep. "I am never going back to my old life. You don't have to worry. Just get better."

Daddy did survive and made his way back to full health. He ended up with a big settlement over the car accident, which helped us all. Everything was going well until the manager of the junkyard propositioned me. I refused his advances, and within a month I was told my services were no longer needed.

Two weeks later, I found another job at a grocery store. I'd worked there for a few weeks when I was hired by a professional exchange, answering calls for several offices and businesses. It turned out, I loved my new job.

CHAPTER THIRTY-TWO

In October 2010, an anonymous donor from my church sponsored me to attend a weekend retreat in Southern California at the Pinecrest Conference Center. It honored me that someone had given me such a great gift, I could hardly wait to get away with my pastor's wife and other women for a time of relaxation and spiritual renewal.

Little did I suspect at the time that I would come face to face with the evil of my past, and God would begin to direct my path to a mission bigger than myself. I left that conference with a burning desire to save my friends on the street but not a clue as to how I would do it.

But God did.

By the time I left the Pinecrest Women's retreat, my mind raced a hundred miles a minute. I struggled to come to grips with all that had been revealed to me in those few days—the deeper truth about my past and what had happened to me. When I returned home, I searched the internet and studied everything I could find about human trafficking. I read the Scriptures and spent time on my knees every day, praying and asking for direction. I learned that a college degree in Human Services was important, so I signed up for classes at Fresno City College. A friend at the retreat had given me a copy of *The Circle Maker* by Mark Batterson. I wouldn't read it until January.

God had given me a desire to help the women on the street, but I needed to help myself first. I told everyone who would listen about sex trafficking and that something needed to be done. The women on the street were not there by choice. They needed help to get out of that life. But there was no place for them to go.

The response was always basically the same: "That's nice." I felt like I was being patted on the head like one would a puppy. No one took me seriously. I wasn't even sure God knew what He was doing. After all, who was I? Someone who'd spent eight years working on the street, pushing sex and drugs. Why would God want to use someone like me? I wasn't qualified. I was sure that's what everyone was thinking.

But I knew what God had put on my heart.

A vision began to form in my mind. I saw a home where women bound by the chains of trafficking and drugs could go to get off the streets. A program to help women transition into a new life. But after months of wishing and sharing my plan with everyone I came in contact with, there was no movement, and no one offered to help.

The only thing I knew to do was to pray. So, I did. *God, I'm not getting traction. I'm doing this alone. Help me, please.*

I still went to work at the exchange. One day I answered a call for Child Protective Services (CPS). When I heard the frantic caller, I knew right away it was Charlie, but he didn't recognize me. He said he was looking for his infant son, who had been put in protective custody the night before. I told him I would leave his message with CPS Services and someone would contact him that afternoon. I wrote his number down and called him back when I went on break.

Charlie was surprised to learn it was me he'd spoken to on the phone. He told me his girlfriend—my friend Jenny—was still getting high and spending her time out on the streets. "Charlie, I want you to know that I'm praying for you and Jenny. You two need to get out of this lifestyle." He didn't know what to say, which kept the conversation short.

Even before God put it on my heart to help the women on the street, I was a little uncomfortable with my job—nothing tangible, just a stirring in my soul. The people I worked with did not know who I was or what I had done. They only saw me as an outspoken Christian who was hoping one day to work with a Christian organization. Someone suggested I make an appointment with Tom Sommers for job counseling. Tom was well known at the local Fresno Rescue Mission for helping men and women who were trying to get their lives on track. In many ways, that was me.

Tom instantly put me at ease the first time I walked into his office. Our conversation went well, until he said, "Debra, I need to know a little about your criminal history."

I felt as though someone had just punched me in the stomach. I wanted to run. I could not possibly sit there and relay the ugly details of my past. This man was an upstanding Christian. What would he think? After a long pause, I burst into tears. "I spent time in jail for solicitation of sex," I managed to get out.

With my secret revealed, I had nothing to lose, so I blurted out my story. "I now know what happened to me wasn't my fault. I was kidnapped and trafficked." I looked away as I continued. "I had no one to talk to. There were no programs for women like me. I needed counseling, but there was none. A lot of my friends are still out there."

Getting more courageous, I looked him in the eye before declaring, "Fresno needs a place for these women to go and get help. Someone needs to help them."

Tom listened with interest. More importantly, he didn't say, "That's nice," or speak to me in a condescending way. Instead, he leaned over his desk and said, "Why don't *you* do it?"

"I feel God leading me to do that, but how?"

"You need to pray for direction. Pray that someone will come alongside you."

"I'm praying and looking for that person who will walk beside me. I don't think anyone really takes me seriously."

"You have to show them you're serious. You need someone who is stable and can advise you."

Before I left, Tom took my hand and looked me in the eye. "You are an amazing woman, Debra. Let me know how I can help you." I left his office feeling empowered.

But I still needed a partner, so I continued to ask God for help.

CHAPTER THIRTY-THREE

2012

Daddy decided he wanted his house and, more importantly, his freedom back. "I cannot keep putting out money for you. I'll buy you a car, but you need to get your own place," he told me more than once.

"You can't do this to me," I whimpered. "Where will I go?"

He gave me no reply.

My paycheck wouldn't cover all my expenses without Daddy's help. How could I pay full rent? I didn't know what I was going to do. My former ways of making a living were no longer an option. I fell on my knees before God and cried out once again. The year before, I had applied for low-income housing but still hadn't received approval. I really needed it now.

Trust Me, a small voice inside me said. I felt His presence.

Two days later, I found a letter from the housing authority in my mailbox. I'd been approved for Section 8, or low-income housing, that would pay most of my rent. This would allow me to live on my own. My kids and I moved into a beautiful home two weeks later.

2013

Even though my residence was in Fresno, I kept my son in Easton schools to finish his senior year. I attended college, worked, and drove Andrew back and forth to school from Fresno to Easton every day. I'd drop Andrew off, then spend the drive back talking with God.

On one of those times, God reminded me of the prayer walk in jail. It felt right to sponsor one in the streets where Mom and I had once stood to entice men. I was empowered to pray over those streets, anoint them, and take them back from the enemy.

I clearly heard a voice: *Draw your circle.*

"Draw my circle?" I asked out loud.

I felt as if I had no control when I passed my regular turn off on Highway 99. The car seemed to drive itself off at Belmont Avenue. Making a right, my car navigated into the turnabout south of the Fresno Chaffee Zoo. As if controlled by a force beyond me, the steering wheel took a turn at Motel Drive, where I once walked the streets and made a left on McKinley Avenue. Then, the Holy Spirit took over, and I began to speak in tongues. Tears streamed freely down my face. I drove a perfect circle around the area before merging back onto Highway 99. The entire time, I was almost unaware of what I was doing. Then, I drove straight home.

I turned the ignition off, my body shaking uncontrollably. What just happened? I rushed into the house and grabbed my Bible, flipping open to Joshua. My eyes fell on Joshua Chapter 1, Verse 3, and I read:

> *I will give you every place where you set your foot, as I promised Moses. Your territory will extend from the desert to Lebanon, and from the great river, the Euphrates—all the Hittite country—to the Mediterranean Sea in the west. No one will be able to stand against you all the days of your life. As I was with Moses, so I will be with you; I will never leave you nor forsake you. Be strong and courageous, because you will lead these people to inherit the land I swore to their ancestors to give them. Be strong and very courageous. Be careful to obey all the law my servant Moses gave you; do not turn from it to the right or to the left, that you may be successful wherever you go. Keep this Book of the Law always on your lips; meditate on it day and night, so that you may be careful to do everything written in it. Then you will be prosperous and successful. Have I not commanded you? Be strong and courageous. Do not be afraid; do not be discouraged, for the LORD your God will be with you wherever you go* (Joshua 1:3–9).

I pulled out my copy of *The Circle Maker*, given to me at Pinecrest, and read it. My heart flipped with amazement. God told me to *draw my circle*. In my mind, I saw big block letters: MAKE YOUR CIRCLE AND I WILL GIVE YOU EVERY PLACE THAT YOU SET YOUR FOOT.

That day, January 16, 2013, I wrote in my Bible. The Holy Spirit was very clear: *I will give you every place you set your foot. You are in a spiritual battle, and there is an evil stronghold in the area I have given you. This is not about you. It is not about anything you can do. You are first to anoint the territory I have given you.*

There was no turning back now.

♦ ♦ ♦

I was inspired to start with a prayer walk, claiming the territory where Mom and I had been enslaved. It was the beginning. I thought of the many church members who'd stayed by my side for so long even though they knew me as flighty. They saw someone who was high one day and going another way the next. But I knew I was high on joy and no longer in my addiction. They knew me as a woman who didn't keep her word. She said she was going to show up but didn't. They all thought it was cute when I told them I was being called to help women on the streets. I still needed someone to come along beside me, someone to believe in me, but no one came.

It had now been over a year since my time at Pinecrest.

♦ ♦ ♦

I decided to attend Church on the Rock, where no one would know me.

At The Rock, a Bible study on the heart of David and Nathan caught my attention. It was held at the home of Tiffany, who was over women's ministry. I decided not to share much about my past. I didn't want them to judge or treat me differently, as I knew they would.

In the Bible, Nathan came alongside David to help him. I needed someone like Nathan. I heard God say, "I am preparing someone to help you. I am sending you your Nathan." The Wednesday night Bible study had met just two weeks. I couldn't hold back any longer. I told my ugly story—or, most of it. A sense of disbelief overcame me. What had I just done? I'd told the very thing I vowed not to tell. I was going to be banned.

But I didn't stop there, I told them about my vision of helping girls who are out on the streets. "God laid it on my heart to start prayer walks and start a ministry." Even as I spoke, I hesitated, fully expecting to hear, "That's nice." I boldly continued anyway. "When I was set free from trafficking, there was no place to go. Only one woman helped me change my ways, Mrs. Hoard. We need to find a safe place for these girls to go."

Tiffany stared at me, not saying a word. My heart dropped. I could barely walk out of the house before bursting into tears. I was sure I'd just blown it.

The next night was Thursday church. I was anxious all day, not knowing what to expect when I got there. When I arrived, Tiffany stood at the door waiting for me. I almost turned around and ran, but Tiffany's eyes were fixed on me.

"Debra, I need to talk to you."

TIFFANY

CHAPTER THIRTY-FOUR

Tiffany's Story

The phone rang. Mom answered. Moments later, she let out a scream and fell to the floor, crying hysterically.

"Mom, what's wrong?"

She didn't reply but dialed a number and yelled to the person on the other end, "Come!"

Our neighbor came over and took my sisters and me into our room. "Stay in here," she said. "Everything is fine. A friend of your mother's passed away, that's all."

That day stays clear in my mind, as if it happened yesterday. I was nine years old and had never seen my mother so upset. Sometime later I learned that my biological dad, Mark, had committed suicide. That moment in time changed my mother's life—and mine.

Mother became pregnant with me when she was sixteen. My father was only fifteen and begged Mom not to let his family know. She made the decision to honor his wishes. When Mom finished high school, she married someone else. Her husband adopted me, and I had always believed he was my real father. Up until Mother answered that call, life was normal.

Except for my secret.

A family member sexually abused me. It started when I was four, but I was too young then to know I should tell. I just knew I didn't like it, and I cried when he approached me.

When Mom was in high school, she had a baby to care for. She didn't hang around after school and on weekends with her friends, who did drugs. When she attended Mark's funeral, she reconnected with some of them. They introduced Mom to the very thing that could numb her pain and destroy her life in the process.

Getting high became more important to Mom than anything else. I was age nine and four years older than my next sibling. Mother left, and I was forced to assume responsibilities not meant for a young girl. This included cooking, cleaning, and caring for my sisters. It was my life.

My stepfather was heartbroken, which caused him to disconnect from the world, including his girls. Since I was the oldest, much of the responsibility fell to me. I cried myself to sleep most nights, wondering why Mom had left me. Why didn't she want me? What had I done? I felt abandoned. I *was* abandoned.

When I entered my pre-teens, I became frustrated and a bit rebellious. I longed for my mother. When I became a teenager, she agreed to let me live with her. I felt as if my adopted dad was glad to let me go.

My life turned from bad to worse. Mom often left me in the care of her friends, and she disappeared for days and sometimes weeks at a time.

"I'll be back soon," she promised as she walked out the door.

I became a convenient babysitter for those I stayed with. Food was scarce. I was given drugs to keep me compliant and doped up.

My calls to Mom were never answered or returned. I had to figure things out on my own. And I did.

I was a perfect target. Those involved in drugs and other illegal activity sought me out for their own needs. Grown men lured and tricked me into being alone with them to have sex. I sometimes felt obligated because they fed me or bought me things I desperately needed. This continued for several years. Some men were three times my age. I thought it was all normal. I later learned what they did to me was illegal. Adults, who should have protected me, put me into dangerous situations. I was a child, and I was trafficked—tricked and guilted into sex acts for food or things.

By the time I turned seventeen, I was addicted to drugs. I did it all—meth, crack, marijuana, and topped it all off with cigarettes and alcohol. Desperate for love, I fell into a relationship with a man in his twenties who beat me, raped me, and mentally abused me. I became pregnant but left him and married a man my mother's age. That lasted a few months and then I left him for a drug dealer who was much older than me.

I thought I had a good plan. I sold drugs to support my habit, bringing my young daughter along when I met with customers. When she was eleven months old, the police raided our house, and the authorities took her. My boyfriend and I were arrested for dealing drugs. I sat behind bars three days before I bailed out and got my daughter back.

When I missed my court date, the police raided my home again. This time Child Protective Services kept my daughter. I ended up in jail, with no bail, for three months. On my daughter's first birthday, I laid on my bunk most of the day depressed, feeling sorry for myself, and refused to eat. There was no one else to blame but me.

In jail, I began to think about my life and what I was doing to my child. I made a commitment to do better by her and not allow what happened to me to happen to her. But once I was released, I went back to the same stuff. It seemed to be an endless cycle.

It didn't take long after I was released to get pregnant again. The judge had warned me that to get my daughter back I needed to complete an in-patient drug program. I found a program—six-month inpatient and six-month outpatient— that would accept me in my condition. I made the choice to take this program seriously, no matter how hard it was.

My daughter was released back into my custody, and my second daughter was born. I enrolled in school, earned my GED, and started college. My boyfriend ended up in prison, which probably helped me keep focused. I was determined to show my girls a better life. I didn't want them to spend their childhood like their mother had, with no stability. It was imperative to protect my girls and keep them out of the hands of men who would do them harm. They needed to feel safe, and it was my job as a parent to make sure they did.

In 1999, I met my current husband and father of my twin daughters—the last children I would have. My new husband was controlled by his addictions and proved to be mentally, emotionally, and physically abusive. We spent nine years of our marriage in turmoil.

One day he became violent, endangering the lives of our children. The police arrested him and charged him with felony domestic violence and child endangerment. My twelve-year-old daughter was subpoenaed to testify against him. Once my husband found that out, he pled guilty and was sentenced. He couldn't bear to see her go through any more anguish because of him.

While in jail, my husband attended Bible studies and church. His heart began to change. In time, so did mine. Our marriage, family, and lives were restored.

As time went on, my empathy for women struggling with addictions grew. Memories of loneliness, despair, abandonment, and unworthiness kept playing in my mind. The only thing I felt good for back then was sex. Driven by an obsession to help women who had been abused by men as I once was, I asked God what I could do to help. I'd found freedom in Christ and wanted others to know and receive what I had.

I donated when our church sent money to support a home in Guatemala for victims of sex trafficking, but I wondered if there wasn't more I could do. Realizing there was a problem right in my own community, I felt compelled to drive down the streets of Fresno where women stood waiting for men to pick them up. What were they feeling? Watching them, the memories of worthlessness rushed into my mind. Those women needed to know there is a God who loves them. They are worth more than they can imagine. I had hope to offer. My desire to help them grew, but I still didn't quite know how.

I lead a Bible study in my home on Tuesday nights. A woman, Debra Woods, had recently started attending. When she shared her story and her heart's desire to start an organization to help women on the street, I listened with amazement. I found myself speechless but knew God had arranged our meeting.

The next night at church, I waited anxiously at the door as she walked toward to me.

"Debra, I need to talk to you."

CHAPTER THIRTY-FIVE

Debra

Tiffany's voice held a sense of excitement. Did she want to talk to me? Why? Was it about what I'd told them the night before? I forced a smile as Tiffany pulled me aside.

"I need to tell you something."

I hesitated, wondering what was on her mind. "Okay."

"I have a big burden on my heart to help those who are caught up in human trafficking. Our church is supporting a human trafficking organization called The Ahikiam Home in Guatemala, and that's wonderful, but I have come to realize trafficking is alive right here in Fresno, California." Tiffany bit her lip before continuing. "I drive down Motel Drive every day and see women walking the streets. My heart breaks for them."

"Really?"

"God has laid it on my heart to help you."

I was stunned. Unable to speak. A glimpse of hope rose in my heart. Could Tiffany be the one?

Up until now, all I'd heard was, "Your story is great. What you want to do is great." But no one was willing to help me. Tom Sommers told me someone would come along who would have a passion for helping me. In Bible study, we learned God sent Nathan to help David. Had He sent Tiffany to help me?

Several days later, I asked God if Tiffany was the one. I prayed, "Show me if she is meant to be my Nathan." The second I finished my prayer, the phone rang. I didn't recognize the number, but I answered anyway.

"Hi Debra, this is Tiffany. I can't stop thinking about our discussion to help women who are on the streets against their will—which is pretty much all of them. There is one thing you need to know though. I was sexually assaulted as a child and into my teens. I understand."

We agreed to meet at a coffee shop the next day. It seemed logical that we find out everything we could about sex trafficking as well as human trafficking. Tiffany brought her laptop computer with her. We researched to see if there might be a local class or conference we might attend.

"Look at this." Tiffany's eyes filled with excitement as she turned the screen toward me. "There's a meeting being held in two weeks right here in Fresno." I studied the details and costs. The human trafficking organization, Made for Them, was sponsoring the event.

"I can't believe it!"

"Can't believe what?" Tiffany shook her head.

"I know the guest speaker, David Fries."

"Who is he?"

"He's the officer who helped me when I was on the street. He listened to me and always seemed to care."

We didn't hesitate. We signed up online right then. After about an hour of excited chatter, we finally parted, anxious to find out more.

The next morning, I couldn't stop thinking about Officer Fries. Would he remember me? I was sure he wouldn't. When I couldn't stand it anymore, I picked up the phone and dialed the non-emergency number to The Fresno Police Department. When the operator picked up, I said, "I would like to talk to David Fries."

"We don't have anyone with that name," came the reply. "Spell the last name."

"F-r-i-e-s, as in French fries."

"Oh. You mean Detective Fries, pronounced *freeze*. I'll put you through."

My cheeks warmed. I had only seen his name on his badge. I'd never known how he pronounced it.

Moments later, he answered the call. "Detective Fries."

"You probably don't know who I am, and this is going to sound totally crazy, but I think I know you."

"Who are you?"

"Debra."

Before I could say, Woods, his voice became full of excitement. "Debra *Woods*?"

"Yes! It's me."

"I can't believe it's you. How are you?"

After a few minutes of catching up, I told him I'd be attending his workshop. "I got excited when I saw your name and wanted to connect with you beforehand."

"Debra, I have been thinking about you and wondering what happened to you. You are one of the reasons I'm on the Human Trafficking Task Force."

I told him what I was trying to do. We talked a good fifteen minutes. Before hanging up, he said, "I'm so glad you called."

"Me too." I felt like I had just been handed a sign, a gift from God in the form of Detective David Fries, pronounced *freeze*. I was on a high, but much better than any high I'd experienced on drugs. I could hardly wait to see him.

I later learned Detective Fries was so excited by my call, he went into Sergeant Chastain's office, who headed the task force, and blurted out, "Guess who called me?"

CHAPTER THIRTY-SIX

Breaking the Chains was the perfect name for our organization. That is exactly what we wanted to do—break chains. But we had nothing and needed guidance on how to start. I arranged a meeting with the Director of Central California Recovery Center, Dale White. In addition to giving us ideas on setting up our program, he helped us apply for our nonprofit status with the Internal Revenue Service. We received approval a couple of months later—unheard of.

The second weekend in May of 2014, Tiffany's church sponsored us to go to a human trafficking retreat at Mount Hermon in the woods of the Santa Cruz mountains on the Central California coast. We met others who were heavily involved in dealing with human trafficking and had their organizations up and running. One leader, I will call Bill, helped us connect with others. He was a very nice man but displayed characteristics like some of the pimps I knew. He was a fast talker who often interrupted, charismatic, smart, and sharp. My stomach churned when I was around him. I couldn't bear to look him in the eye.

On the second day of the retreat, Tiffany and I ate lunch with some of our new friends and discussed what curriculum we might use when we started classes for our girls. After we finished eating, Bill blurted out a suggestion. "Hey, let's go back to my room, and I'll show you how it's done. We'll role play."

Everything inside of me froze. Why was this man inviting me back to his room? Show me how it's done? He wants to have sex with me. Everyone was getting up from our table to leave, but I hung back—frozen.

Tiffany walked away and looked back. "Everything all right, Debra?"

"We can't go with this guy."

"Why?"

"We can't go back to his room and role play or have sex with him." My eyes became teary.

"No, he didn't say that. We're going to his classroom, not his cabin."

"Are you sure?"

Tiffany gave me a reassuring smile. "Yes, I'm sure."

I reluctantly followed her to the conference room where the others were already waiting. I was so embarrassed, that I was unable to participate. *I'm so stupid. So dumb. Lord, how are you going to use* me*—a fool.*

♦ ♦ ♦

I met Arien through Made for Them, an organization that supports those who are survivors of human trafficking victims. Arien is a sex trafficking survivor, and she quickly became one of my best friends and advocates.

ARIEN

CHAPTER THIRY-SEVEN

Arien's Story

When I was a senior in high school, Mother allowed me to go live with my grandparents. Their house was always a respite from the chaotic atmosphere at home. Life was good there. They allowed me to play sports, and after I graduated from high school with a decent grade point average, I started college.

In 2006, social media changed life for me, as it did for thousands of teenagers. It started with Myspace, a place where I could be myself and tell the world my problems. I did just that. I wrote about the pain of my existence and that nobody cared about me.

Little did I imagine, someone was reading, taking notice of this naive and sad girl.

He said his name was Barton. He'd noticed me on Myspace. *You're such a pretty girl. You're special. You shouldn't be alone. How about me taking you out and treating you like the beautiful woman you are?* Thrills ran through my body as I read his words. Without thinking, I said yes. No one had ever paid me this kind of attention.

He arranged to pick me up at the college I attended. My eyes widened as they fixed on his beautiful, late-model, black sports car. I had never seen a car like it, but I knew it must be very expensive. His flattery easily drew me in. *This guy wants to take me out? This guy thinks I'm beautiful? And this guy is handsome too?*

The next few weeks, I lived a dream and fell in love. Barton treated me like I was the only girl in the world. Everything seemed fresh and new. I relished the attention. He took me to expensive dinners, movies, shopping for new clothes, and to get my nails done. Barton paid for everything, and I loved every minute of it. I didn't think to ask how he made so much money.

I didn't question him when he asked, "Why are you still on Myspace? Are you still looking?"

"No, I love you."

"Baby, I want you to close your account."

I cheerfully did as he asked. We were a couple.

After we dated several weeks, Barton took me to dinner and introduced me to Cherry. "She's a friend," he said. Cherry wore fancy clothes and drove a car like Barton's. I liked Cherry. She was friendly and complimented me. Feelings of acceptance and love lured me in.

Sitting on the opposite side of the table, Cherry looked me in the eyes. "You're a pretty girl, Arien. I can help you make a lot of money."

"What's the point of a pretty girl like you making minimum wage and giving half of it to the government?" Barton put his arm around me. "You can work for us, and no one will take anything."

My eyes dashed between them. "Doing what?"

"Entertaining," Cherry said. "It's fun. You'll meet a lot of men who will treat you well."

"Entertaining men?" Something didn't seem right, although I had no idea what she was talking about. "I don't think I can do that. I'm in school."

"You can stay in college. You'll make a lot more money than working at a fast food place, and you wouldn't have to depend on your grandparents anymore," Barton said.

"I don't think so..." A nervous twitch grabbed my stomach.

Barton took me home that night, but he didn't kiss me goodnight. I felt something was wrong. He didn't call for over a week. When I couldn't stand it anymore, I punched in his number on my cell phone. When he picked up, I asked, "Why haven't you called?"

"I'm trying to help you, but you don't trust me enough."

After a short conversation, I agreed to go out of town with him and promised I would re-consider his job offer. I missed his attention.

When we arrived in Modesto on a motel strip, I immediately saw girls walking the streets alone, in miniskirts and high heels. *That's strange.*

Barton met Cherry in front of one of the motels. After they talked for a few minutes, he motioned me over. Cherry took me inside her motel room. Pulling a black mini skirt, a silver tube top, and a pair of red high heels out of a bag, she told me to put them on. I did as she said, wondering what I was going to do.

"I have a date set up for you." Cherry looked me over. "Tell him your name is Peaches and make him happy."

I had no clue what was expected until she handed me a few condoms. Was I supposed to have sex with this guy? A light came on in my head, but there was no turning back. I couldn't handle Barton being mad at me, but I didn't understand. Why would he want me to have sex with other guys? Didn't he love me?

When my first "date" handed me a hundred-dollar bill, a rush of excitement shot through me. I had never seen that much money. *I'm rich.* During the sex act itself, I imagined myself on the beach, just like I'd done when I was molested as a child. It made it bearable.

"Barton is going to hold on to your money while you work." Cherry reached for my cash. "You won't be robbed that way." I didn't see Barton after that and never received any of the money.

I learned Cherry oversaw the other ladies in the group and was known as Barton's bottom girl. After two weeks, Cherry introduced me to Candy, another bottom girl. Candy intrigued me. She seemed so sophisticated. I soon realized Cherry had sold me to Candy's pimp, Eddie. Several questions ran through my mind. What had happened? Had Barton really sold me?

Eddie restricted my interactions to my "dates" and his other girls. If I failed to make at least $1,500 a day, Eddie beat me. Once, after two weeks in the Los Angeles County Jail, Eddie picked me up, gave me wipes to freshen up, and said, "You need to get to work."

After a few months of being on the streets and controlled by Eddie, I couldn't do it anymore. I devised a plan in which I'd keep back some of the money I made. When I saved enough, I got on a bus and escaped to my grandparents.

I was grateful to be home, but something seemed different. My experiences on the streets left me lost, unable to cope with life. Without a pimp giving me detailed directions every day, I didn't know what to do. Feeling lonely and secluded, I opened a new account on Myspace. It wasn't long before I started pouring out my problems to a new guy, who called himself Rudy.

Again, I was charmed by the things Rudy wrote me, things I longed to hear. *I live in Las Vegas. I can't believe I missed noticing you. You are gorgeous.* His praise brought me back to life.

Rudy bought me a plane ticket and met me when I arrived. He gave me a full, long kiss on the lips and told me I was beautiful. He didn't act like a pimp, but I immediately knew he was. I figured this was the life that I was meant to lead. I walked with him into my future willingly. It seemed familiar. It felt comfortable.

Rudy was known on the streets as "Magic," because he made things happen. He lived in a big home with his stable of eight girls. I spent three and a half years with Magic, traveling around the country to places like Montana, Washington D.C., and Arizona. He kept all his girls separated and never alone in the house, making it easier to control us. Eventually Magic trusted me enough to make me his bottom girl. I loved being in such an important and favored position. It gave value to my life.

Everything seemed to be going well, despite Magic forcing me to get two abortions, but tensions were building in my thoughts. One night I asked him to give me some front money to play slot machines to snag potential customers. When he told me no, I snapped.

"Then I'm *done*!"

He grabbed my head, twisted it, and pushed me down. He hit me and hit me and hit me around the face. I didn't care if he killed me. Death would be better than the life I led. He punched me multiple times in the stomach. There was no pain, just anger welling up within me. He picked up a golf club and began hitting my legs. I did my best to defend myself. Finally, Magic fell on the floor exhausted.

I managed to pick myself up and run out of the house, fearing for my life. Maybe the one friend whom I dared to see behind Magic's back might help. It was early morning, but I called her anyway. She agreed to pick me up down the block from the house.

But it didn't take long for Magic to recover and find us.

I pointed anxiously out the side window of the car. "There's a police officer. Pull over."

When the officer saw me, he asked, "Who did this to you?"

I froze and stared at him before answering. "Uh... my boyfriend."

He crossed his arms over his chest. "Someone has really hurt you, but it wasn't your boyfriend. I wish you'd let me help you. Who really did this?"

"It was my pimp."

I agreed to go with the police and tell them everything I knew about Magic, or whatever his name was. I testified against him in court, but he was released the same day. A Las Vegas detective promised me if I testified against Eddie, the police would help me get back to Fresno, but that didn't happen because of a legal issue. Afraid Magic might stalk me and with no place to go, I lived in fear. I lived on the streets and alone, always watching.

By Christmas of 2011, I was exhausted. I called my grandparents. They hired a lawyer to help bring me home. My grandparents were key in my rescue. They never once hesitated to help. They never once judged me. They gave me unconditional love. They spent a good amount of their retirement money to bring me home and helped me through my trauma. I could go on listing all the things they did for me, but most importantly I had their prayers. I'd lived deep in a dark, twisted world and knew I could have lost my life. I truly believe I wouldn't be alive today if it weren't for my grandparents.

Growing up, my grandparents did their best to take me to church, but Mom wouldn't allow it. When I came home from Las Vegas, after everything I'd experienced, the total darkness that engulfed my life overwhelmed me. I needed help. I tried to put my life back together on my own but found it impossible. No amount of alcohol, medication, or counseling worked. But the day I accepted Jesus into my heart and life, a light inside of the darkness shone brightly. I used the light every day to battle the demons that visited me, and continue to visit me to this day, however less often and less vividly.

I found support through a local nonprofit, Made for Them. The director introduced me to Debra Woods and Tiffany Apodaca, who had just started Breaking the Chains, an organization to help sex trafficked victims. I walked with them on their first prayer walk.

Update: Today, Arien sits on the board of Central Valley Justice Coalition and serves as a community advocate. She is the lead victim advocate for Breaking the Chains, a small group leader, and facilitates classes to heal trauma. Arien speaks at high schools and other groups on sexual abuse awareness and prevention. God uses her to prevent other girls from becoming victims, like she once was.

In addition to her involvement with groups to stop sex and human trafficking, she is finishing her college degree in social justice. Being in a place to mentor and help other women who are stuck in or coming out of a similar situation has been rewarding in the sense that, despite how horrible her experience was, she can now use it for good.

Because of her work with sex traffic victims, Arien was awarded a new home from Habitat for Humanity in 2017. In 2018, Arien traveled to Washington D.C. to receive The Eva Murillo Unsung Hero Award from the Congressional Victims' Rights Caucus.

CHAPTER THIRTY-EIGHT

The Fall of Jericho

> *Now when Joshua was near Jericho, he looked up and saw a man standing in front of him with a drawn sword in his hand. Joshua went up to him and asked, "Are you for us or for our enemies?" "Neither," he replied, "but as commander of the army of the LORD I have now come." Then Joshua fell facedown to the ground in reverence, and asked him, "What message does my Lord have for his servant?" The commander of the LORD's army replied, "Take off your sandals, for the place where you are standing is holy." And Joshua did so.*
>
> *Now the gates of Jericho were securely barred because of the Israelites. No one went out and no one came in. Then the LORD said to Joshua, "See, I have delivered Jericho into your hands, along with its king and its fighting men. March around the city once with all the armed men. Do this for six days. Have seven priests carry trumpets of rams' horns in front of the ark. On the seventh day, march around the city seven times, with the priests blowing the trumpets. When you hear them sound a long blast on the trumpets, have the whole army give a loud shout; then the wall of the city will collapse, and the army will go up, everyone straight in." So Joshua son of Nun called the priests and said to them, "Take up the ark of the covenant of the LORD and have seven priests carry trumpets in front of it." And he ordered the army, "Advance! March around the city, with an armed guard going ahead of the ark of the LORD." When Joshua had spoken to the people, the seven priests carrying the seven trumpets before the LORD went forward, blowing their trumpets, and the ark of the LORD's covenant followed them. The armed guard marched ahead of the priests who blew the trumpets, and the rear guard followed the ark. All this time the trumpets were sounding. But Joshua had commanded the army, "Do not give a war cry, do not raise your voices, do not say a word until the day I tell you to shout. Then shout!" So he had*

the ark of the LORD carried around the city, circling it once. Then the army returned to camp and spent the night there. Joshua got up early the next morning and the priests took up the ark of the LORD. The seven priests carrying the seven trumpets went forward, marching before the ark of the LORD and blowing the trumpets. The armed men went ahead of them and the rear guard followed the ark of the LORD, while the trumpets kept sounding. So on the second day they marched around the city once and returned to the camp. They did this for six days. On the seventh day, they got up at daybreak and marched around the city seven times in the same manner, except that on that day they circled the city seven times. The seventh time around, when the priests sounded the trumpet blast, Joshua commanded the army, "Shout! For the LORD has given you the city! The city and all that is in it are to be devoted to the LORD. Only Rahab the prostitute and all who are with her in her house shall be spared, because she hid the spies we sent. But keep away from the devoted things, so that you will not bring about your own destruction by taking any of them. Otherwise you will make the camp of Israel liable to destruction and bring trouble on it. All the silver and gold and the articles of bronze and iron are sacred to the LORD and must go into his treasury."

When the trumpets sounded, the army shouted, and at the sound of the trumpet, when the men gave a loud shout, the wall collapsed; so everyone charged straight in, and they took the city. They devoted the city to the LORD and destroyed with the sword every living thing in it—men and women, young and old, cattle, sheep and donkeys. Joshua said to the two men who had spied out the land, "Go into the prostitute's house and bring her out and all who belong to her, in accordance with your oath to her." So the young men who had done the spying went in and brought out Rahab, her father and mother, her brothers and sisters and all who belonged to her. They brought out her entire family and put them in a place outside the camp of Israel.

Then they burned the whole city and everything in it, but they put the silver and gold and the articles of bronze and iron into the treasury of the LORD's house. But Joshua spared Rahab the prostitute, with her family and all who belonged to her, because she hid the men Joshua had sent as spies to Jericho—and she lives among the Israelites to this day. At that time Joshua pronounced this solemn oath: "Cursed before the LORD is the one who undertakes to rebuild this city, Jericho: "At the cost of his firstborn son he will lay its foundations; at the cost of his youngest he will set up its gates." So the LORD was with Joshua, and his fame spread throughout the land (Joshua 5:13-6:27).

♦ ♦ ♦

Community Prayer Walk

Tiffany and I had lots of faith and not much else. With the help of the Fresno Rescue Mission and The Rock church, we planned our first community prayer walk. Flyers were handed out to as many churches in Fresno that might help.

On the morning of May 31, 2014, we met in front of the Fresno Rescue Mission. Tiffany and I were ecstatic when over 200 people showed up. The biker club, Soldiers for Jesus, stood out among us. The first known Fresno County human trafficking victim and Arien showed up to walk beside us too. Before setting off, we gathered together and prayed that all chains of bondage would be broken. We asked God to free all the women on the streets. We felt aggressive as if we were preparing for a spiritual fight. And we were. The power of the Holy Spirit worked within us and exhibited a strong presence. On that day, nothing could beat us down.

I saw my friend, Jenny, out walking the streets as we marched. It brought tears to my eyes to realize I was free, but she was still in bondage. Rage rose within me remembering what evil men had done to me and what they were doing to Jenny and others I knew. As I walked, I thought of Joshua and the battle of Jericho. I could see the images of the prayer walk at the jail. I saw myself walking and praying around the jail. I saw myself turn off at Highway 99 the day I claimed my territory. When the walk ended, I knew God was going to do something even bigger than I could imagine.

God, bring Jenny to me, I prayed.

JENNY

CHAPTER THIRTY-NINE

Jenny's Story
Breaking the Chains' first intake survivor
"Have you heard about Little Debbie?" a friend asked. "Debbie's got religion. She's off the streets and is starting a program that's supposed to help girls like us."

"What? No way." I couldn't believe what I'd just heard. My friend Debbie had been famous on the street. She acted like she *wanted* to be out there. We'd walked Parkway together for a few years, and my boyfriend, Charlie, had protected us from other pimps. But the last time I saw her, she'd said she wanted to get off the streets.

It had been several years since I'd seen or heard from her. She'd long ago disappeared, and I had no idea what had happened to her.

How could it be that she'd changed this much?

Daddy worked hard to provide a life for me. Mom was absent, mostly due to her love of drugs and crime, which earned her time in prison throughout my childhood. Daddy was always there for me, but I missed my mom. I often wondered why she didn't love me. I wondered what I had done that made her leave. My little girl heart had a big hole in it that only my mother could fill. The truth is, she abandoned all her five children.

When I was sixteen, my older sisters invited me to join them at parties. They introduced me to acid and weed. It was the cool thing to do, but I liked the taste of alcohol even more. My habits affected my school work, and I dropped out in the tenth grade.

I managed to survive with Daddy's help. At the age of twenty, I became pregnant and gave birth to my first son. More money was needed to support my child, but I wasn't sure what I could do to generate more income.

I stepped on the stairs to get on a bus when I noticed a sign on a telephone post nearby. DANCERS WANTED. Dancers? I could do that. I loved to dance.

I called the number. Two men came to my home and interviewed me. They ask me to dance for them and hired me on the spot. The men even took me to get my license to dance and, soon, I was hired for parties. I loved the attention I received. I loved the cash even more.

I danced at local bars in a small town. I made great tips, but some customers wanted more. They would give me their business cards and ask me to meet them after work. They paid handsomely for my "services." It gave me an idea, which I shared with my boyfriend, Charlie. That's when I decided to sell myself on the streets. I soon found there were other men—pimps—who tried to steal me. Charlie stood six foot five inches and weighed two hundred and fifty pounds—all muscle. He easily intimidated anyone who even looked at me wrong. I was left alone. Charlie protected Debbie too. She sometimes gave him money for protection. Charlie and I were in a relationship, which resulted in the birth of our son—my second.

The money was good. The work was grueling. I made $100 per customer plus tips and serviced fifteen to twenty dates a day. Up at six a.m., I worked until nine p.m., seven days a week. Rarely did I take a day off. This was my life—day after day, week after week, month after month, and year after year—for eight years. Thinking back, I realize what a sad existence I lived. There was such an emptiness inside me. I never celebrated a birthday or holiday, including Christmas.

I often wandered into neighborhoods and stared into windows, watching families eating dinner or celebrating a special occasion together, and longed for a life like that. I watched as a couple fought, and I shouted in a whisper, so they couldn't hear, "You're so lucky to have your life. If you're unhappy, you shouldn't be. I would trade places with you in a heartbeat."

Charlie chose to leave the lifestyle and put our son first in his life. I stayed with what I knew. He left with our son, but I knew he still cared. I was eventually lured to Los Angeles with another guy who pimped me. I was arrested over 30 times in Fresno and Los Angeles. Once, while I was under the control of my pimp, I spent seven days in jail. It was during this time I remembered an important part of my life. When I was a child, Daddy allowed me to go to church. I loved church. There were kids to play with and music. Best of all, I felt loved by my Sunday School teachers. This is where I learned about Jesus. I began to pray for God to get me out of my miserable life, especially out of the control of the men who were holding me hostage.

When I got out of jail, I thought my pimp would take me back to Fresno, but he didn't. Four days later, I was arrested again, this time spending ten days in jail. I continued to pray for a way out. I felt God speak to me and tell me everything was going to be all right.

I called a past "date" who said he would help me escape. He agreed to wire money that I could pick up at the Western Union station when I got out. I hoped my pimp would change his mind about taking me back to Fresno. I was prepared in case he wouldn't.

♦ ♦ ♦

A tall, thin, older lady greeted me as I stepped outside of the county jail after being released. She smiled and handed me a bag of clothes and some soup. I smiled back. "Thank you," I told her, grateful for the gifts and her encouragement.

A cab driver pulled up. "Do you need a ride?"

"Yes, but I don't have money."

Without saying a word, he drove off. A few minutes later, he came back. "Get in. Today it's on me." I smiled. *Thank you, God.* There were still kind people in the world. The cab driver drove me where I told him to go. Back to my pimp.

I wanted to go home, but it was made clear that I wasn't going back to Fresno. When my pimp fell asleep, I snuck out of the room and made my way to the Western Union station. The money was there. With cash in hand, I went to the bus station and waited several hours for the bus to leave, scared I would be found.

Once in Fresno, I knew I couldn't call any friends who were doing drugs. Over twenty days clean, I didn't want to take a chance. I remembered what I'd heard about Debbie and the work she was doing in Fresno. My goal was to find her. I believed she might help me. Since Charlie had cleaned up his life and was no longer involved in criminal activity, I called him and asked him to help. Three days later, I met with Debra. I was finally safe.

Little did I know, Debra had been praying for years that I would call. I had been praying just twenty-one days, and God had already answered my prayers. Today, I live in the beautiful Breaking the Chains home. I'm enrolled in school and earning my high school equivalent degree. More importantly, I have received Christ as my personal Savior and have been baptized. I value the support of my church, mentor, the staff, and the programs offered at Breaking the Chains.

Mother received Christ shortly after I did. She's been drug-free for several years now. My heart leaped with joy when one day she told me, "I'm so proud of you, Jenny. I prayed God would allow me to see you turn your life around." Emotion filled me, causing tears to slip from my eyes. I love my mother, and I now know she loves me.

Both of my sons live with their fathers while I heal. I look forward to the day I will live like the families whose houses I used to pass by. With the help of God, Debra, and those who surround me with love, I know I will make it.

Debra with Aunt Terry

Debra's kindergarten picture

Debra at twelve-years-old

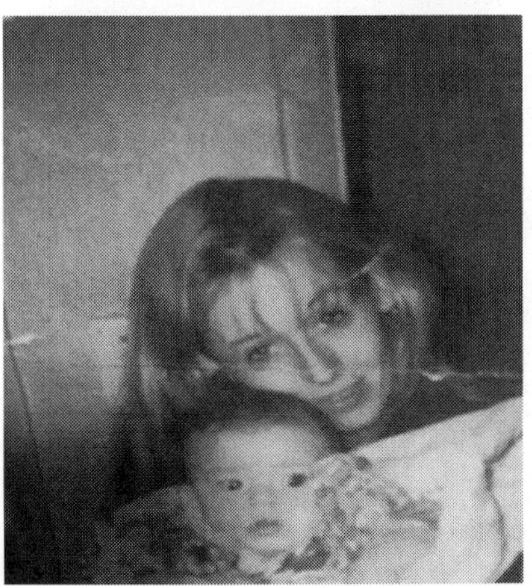

Debra, age twenty-four, and baby daughter

Debra with her daddy, J. R., and brother, David

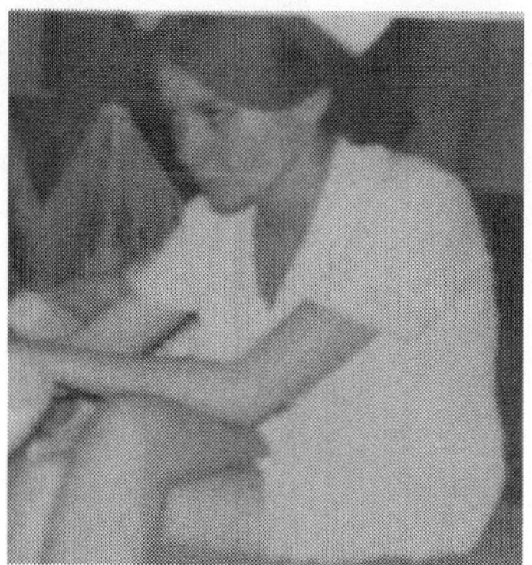

Debra's mom

Grandma and Grandpa Woods

Debra's mom with Sharon Hoard

Debra's first painting from chains to freedom

Debra and Tiffany Co-founders of Breaking the Chains

Daddy (JR) proudly preparing to walk his daughter, Debra, down the aisle

Mr. and Mrs. Mark Rush

Dad singing to Debra while Mark looks on

Perfectly blended family

Debra and Tiffany with Chief Dyer

Debra Rush-California Woman of the year-2018 with Jim Patterson-State Assembly

Tiffany and Debra–offering healing and restoration to survivors of sex trafficking

Debra today

CHAPTER FORTY

Debra

In October 2014, Tiffany answered her phone to hear the voice of a man neither one of us knew. "I understand you need a house. God laid it on my heart to show you one on my church's property."

Taken aback by this generous offer, Tiffany sputtered out, "When can we see it?"

"Would Friday work for you?"

She hung up, and we prayed, "God give us a sign if this is the house."

As we approached the dwelling, my heart dropped to my stomach when I saw the outside. It was a dirty, yellow, unstable looking place sitting on stilts. It had been moved to this location, and who knew how long it had been sitting there, uncared for. It wasn't safe to walk into the house. Standing on her tiptoes, Tiffany looked through a front window. What she saw made her stop in her tracks. A big, beautiful purple wreath hung on the wall, and deep-purple carpet covered the floor. Tiffany's favorite color is purple. She immediately knew this was the house.

Everything inside looked new. It was dusty, and spider webs lined the walls, but it looked in pretty good shape. It didn't make sense. It was so ugly on the outside but beautiful on the inside. Much like the girls we wanted to save. They appear ugly to the world, but inside there is a treasure. God showed me that in my own life.

"We'll take it."

Tiffany nodded. "We can renovate it."

We knew God would have to provide. We didn't have any money. We made a deal with the church that we would refurbish the house, and for the next ten years we could keep it, rent-free. At that time the contract would be reevaluated. Tiffany's uncle owned a large construction company and agreed to do the work for us as a donation. Even though the house looked new inside, it needed a lot of work.

After our nonprofit status was approved, we formed a board, which included Jerilyn, who was a police chaplain, Tina Searcy from the Rescue Mission, Tiffany, and me. We still needed money, offices, and much more, but we had faith that God would come through in a big way. In November, we held our first large event—the groundbreaking for our safe house. But, of course, that provided no financial support for the organization.

To raise money and introduce the public to Breaking the Chains, we decided to hold a banquet. Our event was scheduled for April 23, 2015. I asked God to tell me who was to be the speaker. It needed to be someone who would draw the crowd we needed.

Chief Dyer is going to be heavily involved with Breaking the Chains. Ask him to be your speaker, came the crystal-clear reply. I was wondering if I had heard wrong.

"I don't know Chief Dyer, and he's a very busy man," I said out loud. "Chief Dyer is the chief of police and Fresno is a big city. Why would he agree to talk to me?"

He will be your speaker.

CHAPTER FORTY-ONE

Fall of 2014

Right after the groundbreaking of the safe house, I met with Tom Sommers to update him about the progress of Breaking the Chains and the mission to save women from the streets. "I heard God tell me that Chief Dyer was going to be heavily involved with Breaking the Chains and that I should ask him to be my speaker."

Tom stared at me for what seemed like a full minute. "Let's call him."

Chief Dyer picked up right away. I could hear him say, "What's up, Tom?"

Wow! Tom really does *know him.*

"Chief, I have this lady in front of me. She has a banquet coming up in April. She wants you to be the master of ceremonies."

I heard a chuckle on the other end.

"God told her you would do it."

"What's her nonprofit?"

"Breaking the Chains, a sex trafficking survivor organization."

"When is it?"

"April 23." Tom glanced at me and winked.

"Have her call my secretary after Thanksgiving."

I made the call the Monday morning after the holiday weekend. His secretary, Eileen, took the call.

"May I speak to Chief Dyer? I'm calling to talk to him about being the master of ceremonies at the banquet for Breaking the Chains."

"I'll have to get back to you," she said. A couple of weeks later, I had received no return call. I tried again.

"Chief is very busy. It's the holidays. Can you call after Christmas?"

I tried again the week after Christmas.

"Call back after the first of the year."

The banquet was just a few months away, and I was getting frustrated. I needed to meet Chief Dyer and get his agreement. I decided to try a different approach.

"This is Debra Woods. Before you tell me you'll get back to me, I need to tell you that Chief Dyer is supposed to be the master of ceremonies at my banquet on April 23. I need to talk to him."

"Just one moment." Eileen put me on hold. When she came back on the line, she said, "Honey, I am looking at his calendar. On April 23, it looks like he is master of ceremonies at a human trafficking event."

"That's me!"

"I need to transfer you to Joe Gomez. Chief doesn't handle the details."

I talked to Joe Gomez, and he agreed to fax me a background check form. The next day, Eileen called back and scheduled an appointment with Chief Dyer.

Excited to call Tom and tell him the news, I could hardly punch in his number on my phone. As soon as he answered, I said, "I have an appointment with Chief Dyer!"

Tiffany and I made plans to be at the meeting. Dyer had his people in attendance, including Sergeant Curtis Chastain, the head of the Human Trafficking Task Force, among others. We all sat in a conference room waiting for the chief. After a short time of waiting and chit-chat, a woman stepped into the room and announced, "Chief will be here in a few minutes."

When Chief Dyer walked into the room, everyone focused on him. I bypassed the customary handshake and reached up for a hug. Chief responded by wrapping his arms around me and giving me a quick squeeze. I loved hugging the "top cop." After all the introductions, the chief asked me about my organization. I shared my story about being lured into slavery, my experience with post-traumatic stress events, my arrests, and the sense of hopelessness that overwhelmed me. I told him there was no place for women like me to go. I didn't fit anyone's criteria. It quickly became clear that Chief Dyer was touched by all I shared. "I'll help you any way I can," he said.

I'd found help at last. The Fresno police had always been good to me, but now they were going to help me help other women.

Sergeant Curtis Chastain's Comments

Chief Dyer asked me to attend a meeting with Debra Woods, who said she was starting an organization to rescue women from sex trafficking. She brought along her co-founder, Tiffany Apodaca. I wondered what they would be able to do.

I had reached out to several organizations that said they wanted to help, but usually, their government funding limited who they could take into their program. There was also a lack of understanding of the real problem for women on the streets. I sat in the meeting with a pre-conceived conclusion. I wanted to put Debra in the same category as everyone else. They might have good intentions but were short on deliverables. But, as I listened, there seemed to be something different about her.

Speaking with passion, Debra commanded the full attention of those in the room. It became clear she knew the problems of sex trafficking. Most of those whom I'd reached out to didn't seem to have a full understanding. Debra described how a pimp had lured her, held her, and how she eventually escaped, but there was no place to go for help. She talked about the psychological problems she had suffered, recounted her experiences, and discussed how sedating herself with drugs seemed to be the only thing that took the pain away. She shared how, that with the help of God, she saved her children and herself.

Since she first knew she wanted to start Breaking the Chains, she'd educated herself and used her knowledge and experience to help former prostitutes. Debra asked for the meeting with Chief Dyer for one reason—to ask him to be her master of ceremonies at their first fundraiser.

The chief was clearly moved and agreed to help Breaking the Chains. Somewhere deep inside, I felt this one could make it. I left the meeting hoping she would, but thinking, *we'll see.*

That meeting sparked what would become a long journey with Debra Woods and Breaking the Chains.

CHAPTER FORTY-TWO

Debra

In February 2014, before the first prayer walk, I left my job at the professional exchange and went to work for Rescue the Children—an arm of The Fresno Rescue Mission that serves women and children—as a case manager. The director warned me, "Be careful not to blur the lines of this job and Breaking the Chains." When I was at work, I had to focus on that, and my new venture could not interfere.

I was about to leave work one day when I received the first rescue call. "This is Rescue the Children. May I help you?" The man on the other end was calling from the Rescue Mission and informed me a sex trafficking victim and her baby had walked into their offices and needed help. Breaking the Chains was not yet prepared to take in our first survivor, but the reality was here—ready or not. I knew I couldn't do anything because I was still employed with Rescue the Children, so I called Tiffany.

"We have our first victim, Rosa, who needs our help. You're going to have to take this." I gave her the number of the person who had called me. After hanging up the phone, I texted Detectives Fries and Sergeant Chastain with information on the girl we were about to rescue. They promised backup if needed.

TIFFANY

Tiffany
When I arrived at the Rescue Mission, Rosa was already gone. My cell phone rang shortly after.

"This is Rosa." She spoke in a whispered, shaky voice. "I'm in the restroom of the restaurant down the street. I'm scared they'll find me. Please help me."

"Stay right where you are. We'll be there in a minute. Everything is going to be fine, I promise."

The police task force was in place and ready to move. The team and I quickly converged at the restaurant, but Rosa wasn't in the bathroom. An officer quickly found her holding her son in the trees behind the building. I carefully approached her. "Hi, Rosa. I'm Tiffany. I'm here to help you." The terror in her eyes turned to tears as she rushed toward me. Taking Rosa in my arms, I led her to my car for a trip to a partnering safe house, miles away. Knowing she had a baby, I'd brought a car seat. With the three of us in the car, we started the journey to free Rosa.

The nervousness and horror in her eyes frightened me. Horrified that at any moment those men who had trafficked her and held her and her baby hostage could pull up beside us in the car, I held my phone in my hand, ready to call the police. Relief rushed through me once we were safely at our destination.

I called Debra after I knew Rosa was okay. "We need to make a plan on how we're going to rescue our girls. The police need to assist us. I was terrified all the way here, and now I have to drive back to Fresno—alone."

ROSA

Rosa's Story

I didn't know any services available to me. I had a baby to support, and the only way I knew to make enough money was to sell myself. Little did I know I was being watched by men who realized I worked on my own and wanted to profit from me. One night, as I approached my apartment, three men ambushed me at gunpoint and pushed me through my door. They told me that I was now under their control and would turn over all my money to them.

"We're gonna take care of your son when you're out on the street," one of them said, then laughed. "If you do anything stupid, we'll kill him."

My insides froze. I had to protect my son. Alone and feeling there was no other choice, I did what they wanted.

The next night, one of them came to the apartment to watch my son until I returned the next day. This continued each night, and they always reminded me, "We're watching." I confided my situation to a neighbor I met in the washroom. With her help, we devised a plan to escape. One hot July night, after the men left, I quickly packed a bag. About two in the morning, carrying my baby, I snuck out, leaving everything I owned in that apartment. Tiptoeing my way down the stairs in the dark, peering around every bush, I feared I was being watched from somewhere I couldn't see.

I walked through the bushes from house to house and through apartment complexes until I reached a closed store, two streets down. I hid behind a large, smelly garbage bin in the back. I didn't have to wait long before a car I recognized pulled up. My neighbor's husband motioned for me to get in the back seat. "Stay down," he ordered.

Once I closed the door, he put his foot on the pedal and sped away. "I'm taking you to the Rescue Mission. They'll know what to do."

I held my breath all the way. My rescuer walked me into the building and told the man at the desk, "She needs your help."

"We don't take women in here," came the answer.

"Please help me. There are men out there who want to kill my baby and me," I cried.

The man motioned for me to come in and led me to a small room with a bed where my baby and I could sleep. The next morning, someone came and asked me to follow him to an office where someone might be able to assist me.

I sat at the mission all day telling my story to one kind face after another, while they figured out what to do with me. I learned about the mission's women's program in another part of town, but I didn't fit in there because I wasn't recovering from drugs or prison time. I later found out helping women on the street was a new idea in Fresno. Late in the day, I learned that Tiffany, from Breaking the Chains, was coming. They gave me her cell number. A breath of relief escaped from my lungs, but I remained frightened, scared, distrustful. By the afternoon I was exhausted, paranoid, and afraid. I took my son, left The Rescue Mission, and walked down the street into a restaurant and hid in the bathroom. I called Tiffany and told her where I was.

Fearful that those who'd held me hostage would find me, I couldn't stay still. I left the bathroom and ran and hid behind the trees in the back of the restaurant. Minutes later, police drove up, and one of them noticed me. A young woman got out of the car and started toward me.

"Rosa?"

"Yes?"

"It's Tiffany. You're safe."

I ran toward her and to freedom.

CHAPTER FORTY-THREE

And I will restore to you the years that the locust hath eaten, the cankerworm, and the caterpillar, and the palmerworm, my great army which I sent among you.

(JOEL 2:25)

Debra

In 2013, I met Mark Rush, an associate pastor at Church on the Rock. Our kids were the same age, hung around together, and our lives crossed several times a week. He was my minister and my friend, but nothing more.

On my birthday, July 26, 2016, I found an envelope on my office couch. It was from Mark—a gift certificate for a therapeutic massage. I found it odd, but sweet.

"I hope it isn't too much, and it doesn't freak you out," Mark said, nervously, when I called to thank him.

"No, that's fine." I laughed, amused. "I love it." But why had he given it to me?

Tiffany joked, teasing that he liked me. "No way!" I said. Thoughts of being romantically involved with Mark had never crossed my mind.

A month later, on August 25, Chief Dyer was to be honored for fifteen years as chief of police at an event billed "Gala Evening of Dinner, Dancing, and Entertainment." Tiffany's husband accompanied her, and a girlfriend agreed to come along with me. Five hours before the event, my friend canceled.

Not wanting to go alone, I voiced my disappointment to Tiffany.

"Call Mark," she suggested.

I giggled. "Why?"

"I dare you. Call him."

"Okay, fine. I will."

Mark's phone rang twice before I heard his voice on the other end. I asked him to accompany me. He paused before asking, "Are you sure?"

"Yeah."

"What do I wear?"

Five hours later, Mark walked beside me in a black suit, white shirt, and light-blue tie. He was a fine-looking guy, but I couldn't get distracted. Early in the evening, not giving it a second thought, I left Mark at our table and wandered off to network the crowd.

I was in deep conversation with the new director of the Fresno Rescue Mission when a slight tap on the shoulder disturbed my train of thought. It was Tiffany.

"Where is Mark?"

"Sitting over there." I pointed toward our table.

"You left him by himself?"

"Yeah."

"Oh, my gosh, you are so rude." Tiffany flashed me a look of indignation. "He's supposed to be your date for the night."

"My date? He's not my date." I blinked with surprise.

"He should be with you." Tiffany's eyebrow raised as if I should have known this.

"Okay, if you say so." I realized that maybe I shouldn't have left him alone. Rushing over to Mark, I quickly apologized. "I'm so sorry. You want to walk around with me?"

Jumping out of his chair, he answered quickly, "Yes, I would."

I guess Tiffany was right.

When Chief Dyer strolled into the crowd, I could hardly wait to introduce my date. Two weeks earlier, Chief had told me I needed to find a godly man. *This might impress him.* Grabbing Mark's hand, I rushed over to greet the chief. "Chief Dyer meet Mark Rush, my date. He's a pastor." The words tumbled out. My face grew warm at the condescending tone I heard in my voice. I was so embarrassed.

Chief Dyer shook Mark's hand and looked him square in the eye. "You'd better take care of this one."

Mark turned to me with a grin. "I plan to."

I stared up at him wondering what had just happened. Quick as a flash, something changed in our relationship, but I didn't know what. Strings played somewhere, but they weren't anywhere in sight. The room began to swim, my hands quivered, my heart raced. Did I like this guy? Why was I suddenly feeling anxious? I'd never been nervous around a man in my life.

For the first time, I worried if my makeup looked right, if my clothes were perfect, or if my words were appropriate. *Oh, my gosh, he's looking at me. Why is he telling me about his ex-wife? Awkward.*

After that night, I did my best to avoid Mark. Surely, I'd misinterpreted something. He wouldn't get involved with someone with my past. The church wouldn't allow him to date someone like me. After all, Mark is a pastor. *What's wrong with me?*

On Christmas Day 2016, a mysterious gift sat under my tree. Curious who it was from, I opened it. Inside lay a teddy bear, a bracelet, and a taser? A note read, *For comfort, love, and protection, Mark.*

Mark later told me that, before he sent the Christmas gift, he asked the church board if he could pursue a relationship with me. Kind of old-fashioned, but nice. We spent the next few months getting to know one another and sitting in counseling sessions together. We kept our secret from the world. In January, we announced to our friends, "We're a couple!"

At 3:30 in the afternoon on March 29, 2017, in front of friends and family, Mark knelt, took my hand, and asked, "Will you marry me?"

"Yes, I'll marry you," I replied before tears of joy left me speechless. I felt like Cinderella as he slipped the white gold and diamond ring on my finger.

"I'm going to marry a pastor. I'm going to marry my prince," I told my friends.

CHAPTER FORTY-FOUR

Saturday, March 25, 2017

I found mom slumped in her chair and unresponsive. After the paramedics arrived and assessed her, they took her by ambulance to the hospital. She had overdosed on prescription drugs and methadone, causing her heart to stop for several minutes. The doctor told me Mom was brain dead, which could leave her in a vegetative state. In the hope she might survive, Mom was put on life support.

I called both of my sisters, Christine and Lisa, to tell them that if they wanted to come and say their goodbyes, they needed to get here right away. "We need to make the decision when we might want to pull the plug," I told each of them.

They both assured me that whatever decision I made they would support. Lisa could not get a plane out soon enough, but Christine said, "I'm on my way."

Late in the afternoon, Christine and her husband arrived from Northern California and joined Mark and me at the hospital. After a brief time with Mom, we decided to go to dinner to get caught up on what was happening. We planned to go back after we ate.

As I walked to my car, the weight of the world sat on my shoulders. My heart was crushed in a ball. Defeat filled my soul. The energy was drained from my body. Complete hopelessness pushed me into a depressed state. God wasn't going to save my mother. I had never really had her in this world, and I wasn't going to have her in the next.

After dinner, I told the others, "I'm done. I'm emotionally exhausted. I just need to go home and spend some time alone." Getting out of my chair, I rushed out of the restaurant, crying inconsolable tears from the depths of my soul.

Mark ran after me. After he gave me a minute to catch my breath, he asked, "Do you think it's a good idea not to go back?"

"What do you mean is it a good idea? How could you say that? I'm tired. It's been a difficult day. I can deal with this in the morning."

Mark just listened and then grabbed me into his arms. He cradled me for a minute. "I love you so much, Debbie, but I think you need to go back down and be with your mother. I feel if you don't you will regret this for the rest of your life."

I couldn't speak. My body tightened. How could he say this? He didn't understand how it was with my mother. Running through my mind were all the things that had happened between us since as far back as I could remember. We didn't have the ideal mother-daughter relationship. How could he say *I* would have regrets?

"The enemy doesn't want you to go back. God might give your mom another chance."

Mark finally convinced me to go back. We all went back to the hospital to watch Mom sleep.

♦ ♦ ♦

Mark stood at the foot of Mom's bed, quietly praying her eyes would open. Hope of ever seeing my mother come to know Jesus was nonexistent. Within my heart, anger toward God raged.

I had once believed God would save my mother, but He never had. Every part of my body and mind hurt so much, but I couldn't cry. No prayer came from my mouth. Her chances were over. I wanted to scream, "Mark, just shut up. God isn't going to bring her back. God isn't going to keep his promise to me."

"Mom is moving!" Christine yelled, clearly startled.

As if an angel brushed her face, Mom's eyelids fluttered, leaving me stunned. She smiled up at me from her hospital bed. Not believing what had just happened, I stared for a few seconds before I finally took her hand, looked her in the eyes and said, "I love you." Tears streamed down my cheeks.

After Mark told the nursing staff Mom was awake, she was taken off life support and put on full-flow oxygen, allowing her to talk. Grateful God had given Mom another chance, I wasted no time. "I have a question for you." I swallowed hard. "Do you want to accept Jesus as your Savior?"

"No," she whispered, looking away.

I didn't push.

Mark and I went to see Mom a few days later. After a bit of chit-chat, Mark took Mom's hand, "Do you want to receive Jesus as your personal Savior?" He paused. "It's not too late."

She raised her eyes toward him. "Yes."

Yes? What had changed? She couldn't say yes to me, but she said yes to Mark? After my initial surprise, I allowed joy to fill my heart, but I was not able to speak.

Mom repeated each phrase Mark voiced as he led her in a salvation prayer. She was coherent enough to repeat and respond. I stood there amazed. Mom would be in heaven one day.

God always keeps His promises, even when we give up.

After Mom woke up, I believed she might be okay. The doctor told me he planned to send her to a skilled nursing facility by the end of the following week, optimistic she would continue to gain strength. Confident she was on her way to healing, I allowed my busy life to take over and didn't make it down until Sunday afternoon. Mom seemed a little lethargic but able to communicate.

The next morning, I called to check on Mom. She was fine. But around two o'clock, I answered the phone and recognized the voice from the hospital.

"We need you to come in and meet with medical staffing to discuss your mom."

The social worker greeted me when I arrived at the hospital and asked me to sit down with her and the doctor and nurse.

"I have some bad news," the doctor said, after looking over her chart. "We don't know why, but your mother's body seems to be slowly shutting down. She's incapable of producing or processing oxygen."

My head spun, trying to understand. I'd thought Mom was getting better.

The doctor looked down at Mom's chart and explained that they needed to continue giving her high-flow oxygen. It could only be done in a hospital setting; therefore, she could not be moved to a skilled nursing facility. Looking somber, and as the nurse and social worker looked on, the doctor folded his arms. "We have another option. Put her in a medically induced coma, send her to Intensive Care, and put her back on the ventilator in the hope that her body will heal." The doctor sighed. "Honestly, I don't think she's going to get better. She hasn't eaten all week, and the staff is unable to coax her."

This couldn't be happening. "Is there a third option?"

"Due to her rapidly declining state, put her on hospice care and help her transition to the afterlife."

"But she's awake and alert. I don't understand." Yet, somewhere deep inside, I felt he was right. Although I was the executor and had a medical conservatorship, I was being asked to make a decision I didn't want to make without asking Mom what she wanted. Grateful she was conscious enough to speak, I asked the nurse to go with me.

When I told Mom what the doctor had just shared, she smiled and laughed as if I was joking. "Mom, I'm not joking. We have a serious decision to consider. Do you understand what I'm saying?" I held her hand tighter, fighting the back tears. Almost begging, I rubbed her fingers. "I need you to help me with this."

Mom stared at me with a puzzled expression and then glanced at the nurse. She wasn't getting it. I turned toward the nurse. "Please explain."

Stepping closer to the bed, the nurse peered down at my mother, "Mrs. Arakelian, I'm sorry, there's nothing else we can do for you."

The realization of what was to come hit Mom like a powerful force of the wind. She shook her head, her eyes darting between the nurse and me. Her face turned pale and registered a look of terror. Mom stared at the wall. After a few seconds, she whispered, "Wow. Wow. Wow."

"Mom, I can't make this decision. I need you to tell me what you want me to do." I tried to keep my emotions in check.

She looked at me, and her eyes watered. "I'm tired, Debra, and I don't want to be in pain anymore."

After a long pause, I nodded. "Well, hospice it is." The nurse left us to be alone.

Tears flowed freely, but then Mom suddenly smiled. "Debra, you are so beautiful."

She's never told me that.

Almost immediately, the nurse began administering high levels of pain medication, which continued for the next two days. I sat at Mom's bedside while she slept and went in and out of consciousness.

During her waking moments, we talked about lots of things, but I desperately needed to tell her what weighed heavily on my heart. With a deep breath of courage, I took her hand. "I'm sorry for everything I've said and everything I've done to hurt you." I sobbed, feeling guilty for every fight we'd had, every nasty, hateful name I'd called her, and every bad thought I'd had toward her.

"I know. I'm sorry, too." She held tightly to my hand.

My breath caught, holding back the dam that felt ready to break. Mom had never apologized to me for anything in her life. The closest she had come was when I asked her to watch my kids while I sat in jail. The flood of tears that couldn't be held back came. Mom was crying too. We held on to each other tightly, not wanting to let go. In those moments, I can't explain the love I felt for my mother. I will always treasure those last hours we had together. Maybe, in the end, I hadn't been such a bad daughter. Maybe she did the best she could.

Maybe we both did.

♦ ♦ ♦

Friday, April 7, 2017

When I stopped by to see Mom that morning, she seemed a little goofy, but looked and acted mostly like herself. I didn't believe she was going anytime soon. *Mom's fine.*

At two o'clock that afternoon, I received a call from the hospital. "Come now," a voice demanded.

"Is something wrong?"

"Get here as soon as possible. I think it's happening."

I drove to the hospital at a rapid pace, praying I wouldn't be too late. Mother was asleep but looked peaceful when I entered her room.

"We haven't been able to wake her," the nurse said when she walked into the room. The oxygen had been removed the day before when it became uncomfortable.

For a few minutes, I tried to rouse her, wanting to talk to her one more time. When she wouldn't respond, I used my phone and brought up worship music, hoping that would be calming.

"How long can we expect this to continue?"

"We aren't sure."

Mark was out of town, but I called my friend, Arien, to come and sit with me. Mom wasn't in any pain. I watched her for the next four hours as she dreamed. Occasionally she cracked a smile.

Around seven o'clock that evening, Mom stopped smiling. Sometimes she opened her eyes. For the next hour and fifteen minutes, I watched as her breathing became erratic and then slowed until she took her last breath. It was precisely eight fifteen in the evening when she slipped quietly into the arms of Jesus. Mom seemed at rest, and I already missed her.

After the medical staff did what they needed to do, they left me alone with Mom. I sat with her for the next forty-five minutes, reflecting on my life—on Mom's life—on our lives together. Gratitude filled my spirit as I held her thin, scaly hand for the last time. I was grateful Mom and I had come to terms with the past, grateful I had been the one to care for her in the end, and grateful I would see her in heaven.

That somehow made it easier.

I thought of the weekend when I was a child, and just the two of us stayed in that tiny apartment at the prison. I remembered the closeness I felt and the hope I had when I left. A flood of tears streamed down my face. My heart cried for all that might have been and for all that was lost.

"Oh, Mom." I laid my head on her chest and sobbed.

Thoughts of Piggy, the pit bull mother who lovingly cared for her puppies, and of Squaw, who bit the head off her newborn, entered my mind. Long ago, through this experience, God had helped me to understand why some women were ill-equipped to be good mothers. Maybe my mother was one of those. My own mothering skills had left much to be desired, leaving in question my own children's future. But, through God's grace, He put Grandma, aunts, Sharon Hoard, and others in my life to teach and gently guide me to be the mother I am today. That realization allowed me to forgive Mom long ago.

Forgiving her freed me.

God reminded me that He gave me my mother to fulfill His purpose. God allowed me to be part of bringing Mom to a saving relationship with Jesus. I was the one God used to break chains of bondage for Mom, for me, and now for countless other women.

No one is beyond redemption, I heard somewhere from within. *You're not. Your Mother's not. You are my proof.*

It seemed a fairy tale. I never believed it would come true. But it did. On June 10, 2017, before over 200 family and friends, I married Mark Rush, a pastor and the love of my life. We blended our families. Together, we have seven amazing children. My son Andrew is in college. Kiara is in her last year of high school and looks forward to joining the Air Force. Juliana and Kendra are happy, healthy students.

The chains break here.

CHAPTER FORTY-FIVE

"Debra, there is someone here to see you this morning who needs our help," my assistant announced as I walked into the Breaking the Chains office.

"What's her name?"

"April."

"Where is she?"

"She went to the bathroom and will be right back."

"Bring her in when she returns." I turned the key to my office to get ready for my day. Another woman to save. Always another one to save.

A knock on my door told me April was back. Looking up, I came face to face with a five foot eight, slender body, touting long, thick, messy black hair. She appeared to have not slept in days. The red nail polish screamed out for a fresh manicure, and the circles under her eyes held a hint of a once beautiful girl. Her wrinkled clothes looked much like the ones I once wore when entertaining wealthy men, but more expensive.

"I'm Debra." I offered my hand. The faraway look in her eyes told me she was in no condition, mentally or physically, for formalities.

April stared at me before she broke out in uncontrollable sobs. I took her in a bear hug, allowing her fear to release. "Everything will be all right, I promise."

I pointed in the direction of the extra chair in my office. "Please, sit down." I pulled my chair in front of her. "What can I do for you, April?"

Her body tilted away from me, shoulders hunched over, and arms folded. "I was told you might be able to help me."

"You want to tell me what happened to you?"

"I was a model once, you know." She took a deep breath. "I got an offer that seemed too good to turn down." She paused, blinked a few times, and continued. "I met a man who offered to make me a star, a porn star." She whispered the last phrase, barely able to say the word "porn."

I handed her a tissue. April took it and dabbed her eyes. "It sounded glamorous and exciting. The money was more than I had ever made or seen for that matter. I had every material thing I wanted." I leaned toward her, taking her hands in mine.

"I was made to do things that were ugly, things I can't talk about." April paused for a second. "I've sold my soul to the devil. There's no way out for me."

"I felt that way once too. April, there *is* a way out."

"Really? But no one made me do this. I can't understand how I could have let this happen to me. How could I have done the things I've done?" Her body shook. "I'm so ashamed." Her voice grew louder and angrier as she continued to talk. "It never seemed to be enough. I was asked to do more, taking me deeper and deeper into a world I thought I could never escape. Each time I was made to have sex in front of a camera with men I didn't know, ugliness screamed out from deep within. I'm so ashamed. I'm so ashamed." She cried, shaking her head.

"I know." Taking her into my arms, I held her and gently patted her back. After April regained her composure, I asked her a question, to help me get a sense of her trauma. "What was your life like before you were caught up into porn? What about your childhood?"

April choked up as she told me enough to understand. She revealed she had a tumultuous childhood—a far too familiar story. She suffered from the trauma of abandonment and multiple rapes from various male family members. Add all that to her life in the porn industry, and it was no wonder what I saw before me was a heap of ashes.

Many individuals in the sex industry are experiencing unimaginable trauma on levels we can't even conceive. They need our help. Unfortunately, if the adult victim cannot prove that another human being led them into sex trafficking through force, fraud, or coercion, they are labeled a prostitute. Because they are not viewed as victims, they are not eligible to receive services through a federally or state-funded program.

Porn is simply legal sex trafficking. April was not a minor, and no one made her do it. She did not fit the legal definition of a victim. Therefore, any government-funded agency that deals with human trafficking would not be able to help her. She didn't meet their criteria.

Yet, when April sat before me, I knew that she was as much a victim as I had been. The trauma a woman experiences is not based on how she entered the sex trade or at what age. April had turned to me for help and help her I would. Because Breaking the Chains has experienced tremendous community support in the short time we've been in existence, we can use our resources to help a victim, no matter how she comes to us. Other nonprofits do not enjoy the same backing we do and must rely solely on government funding.

As a society, we need to do more. Breaking the Chains is working with national officials to begin a campaign to broaden the term "sex trafficking" to include the full spectrum of victims: women like April, who have suffered childhood abuse but now find themselves catapulted into the sex industry; children who have been in the foster care system, are now removed and have no place to go, and as adults they feel have no choice but to participate in sex for survival; and any individual whose prior life circumstances became the catalyst that launched them into a seemingly inescapable nightmare.

They all need our help.

As of today, the federal definition of "sex trafficking" has been used as an umbrella term for the act of recruiting, harboring, transporting, providing, or obtaining a person for commercial sex acts through the use of force, fraud, or coercion. The Trafficking Victims Protection Act (TVPA) of 2000 (Pub).

The women we serve on our campus are vetted under one criterion. Have they ever worked in the sex industry at any level? Based on that and that alone, we will provide services.

EPILOGUE

I woke up three hours earlier than normal, my heart hurts for those I truly love and have seen struggling lately. Falling on my knees in prayer, I asked God, "What more can I do? I want to fix their problems. I want to pull them out of their nightmares with a giant rescue net and pull them back to shore. I have tried repeatedly, but it feels like it's never enough. My burden is heavy. God, tell me what to do."

I stayed silent, not offering any more prayers for what seemed like an hour—listening, waiting, hoping God would answer me.

Suddenly, a vision flashed before me. I was reminded that, for fifteen years, my own family kept throwing me a lifeline and pulling me back to shore. But I would never get up and walk off the beach. I laid there exhausted, happy to be out of the water, at least for a while. But then it didn't take long before a wave came and took me back out to sea, back to my tormentors. One day, I almost drowned. That time, no one came to rescue me. I panicked and blacked out.

When I woke up, I lay once again on the shore. Just off in the distance, I felt someone beckoning me to come. With no one to help, for the first time, I began to crawl and drag myself through the sand. As I struggled to move forward, I gained strength, moving faster and faster. Eventually, I stood up and ran and ran. As I got closer, I saw what called me. It wasn't a person. It was a cross. At the base of the cross was a Bible. Attached to the Bible was a giant lifeline.

I opened the Bible, God's Word. As I read, the secret was revealed. My family kept throwing me the only lifeline that could save me—Jesus—but I always turned back. In the end, it was His written Word that touched my heart and mind.

Jesus is the lifeline that will save the women I'm so eager to help. Not me, but God. He answered my prayers, and He will answer theirs.

As a second-generation victim/survivor, I have a unique insight into the world of sex trafficking. Some have asked me how I could forgive my mother for betraying me in so many ways. When I learned her story, I began to realize she was a victim too—a different kind of victim. By federal definition, my mother sold herself by choice. But Mom was horrifically abused, sexually, physically, and emotionally, as a child. At twelve years old, Mom was thrust into a broken foster-care system, and by the time she was thirteen, she was living on the streets.

In Mom's mind, the streets were safer. It was anything but a choice. It was a life catalyst that led her to do the unthinkable. In a short period of time, she was wrapped in addiction and a lifestyle that she would never be able to escape, dying way before her time. So many women on the street have similar stories. I know my mother could never have been a nurturing mother like Piggy, but I am grateful God allowed me to be.

God inspired Breaking the Chains, and today we enjoy full support from law enforcement and the community. We are fully equipped to rescue and provide safety and services to women who once thought there was no help for them. My joy overflows each time I witness the restoration of a woman, knowing God allowed me to be a part of it. And remember Mrs. Martin, the correction officer who prayed with me in jail? She now works for Breaking the Chains.

A FINAL WORD FROM SERGEANT CHASTAIN

Sergeant Chastain
Head of Human Trafficking Task Force
Fresno, California

We are losing our daughters to horrific crimes associated with the sex trade. As a member of law enforcement, I work with community leaders and nonprofits to stand against human trafficking in any form. It is essential to have the right people in the right place to make effective change. Debra Woods is one of those people. She uses her past to expose pimps and help victims of the crime of sex trafficking.

Like every other vice detective in law enforcement circles, at one time I believed that most of the women who worked on the streets, selling themselves, could leave any time they wanted. Therefore, they were treated as if they were willing participants. We felt that the only reason a woman chose to prostitute herself was that they liked the money, loved the pimp, or felt this was temporary to escape something far worse. I look back now and realize how wrong I was. Nothing could be further from the truth. These women are victims, and we need to help them.

It was frustrating to hear that some organizations were interested in helping, but their government funding limited what they could do. Unfortunately, these targeted guidelines did not meet the profile of every woman who needed help. One such example was a pregnant woman with outstanding solicitation warrants in other jurisdictions. She had recently used her drug of choice in an attempt to hide the pain and just get through the night. No one could help her due to funding restrictions. It was exasperating each time I learned a victim didn't meet funding criteria or was excluded due to the conditions a particular organization had in place.

I was disappointed that services for those caught on the street hadn't developed the way I thought they would, but then Debra Woods showed up. In our conversations, Debra told me about one of the detectives in my unit, David Fries. "He had such an impact on how I viewed law enforcement when I walked the streets. He showed compassion and treated me with respect on the numerous occasions that he had contact with me."

Something exciting happened through our combined efforts. The community came together behind abolishing human trafficking and saving victims. God had a plan. Churches contacted me requesting that I speak on what we were seeing in our area. One faith-based group, The Central Valley Coalition, coordinated with other churches and is a leading educational component in our area. Numerous people asked, "What does the community need? How can we help?" The biggest need was for housing and training for those who were exploited in the sex trade industry and returned, time and again, to the streets and their pimps as their only source of income to survive.

Now on the Human Trafficking Task Force, David Fries has been the most successful human trafficking investigator, gaining convictions against pimps and traffickers in state and federal courts. Perhaps his passion started with Debra and the other women he met on the streets. On one occasion, David and I spoke at a men's church group that wanted to learn more about the topic. At the end of David's talk, I walked up, listening as he spoke to a couple of men. His back was turned to me when I overheard him say, "I believe that it is God's plan for me to be where I am today." I continued to eavesdrop as he went on. "I never planned or had a real interest in vice. It wasn't until I got here and saw the difference that is made in the lives of these women."

Exactly, David! I chose and worked to be where I am, but I too believe it was God's plan. I don't think I ever told David what I heard that day, but I wholeheartedly agree with what he said. God assembled the perfect team, which includes Breaking the Chains, to address human and sex trafficking in our area.

The first time I called Debra in to help, I wondered how she would do.

The team and I had been conducting an undercover operation, observing women we suspected to be loitering for the purpose of prostitution. The plan was not to react to the women walking the streets but to see if we could identify who might be controlling them. Playing the role of the usual voyeur john who hangs out in the area, I had the windows down and listened while one girl, dressed for the part, argued with someone on her cell phone. During the exchange, she looked up at a specific motel room as if she was talking directly to someone inside. I let my team know, so they could set up to watch.

I observed a second girl walk up to the room and knock on the door. It was answered quickly by a male, who let her in. The girl we were watching hung up her cell phone, put it away, and went back to looking for a date. She saw me, and we exchanged smiles. She then walked directly over to my car. With my hidden radio, I let my team know what was happening, allowing them to monitor our conversation through a concealed wire. The girl and I made an agreement for a sex act and the amount of money she would get. She jumped into the car and directed me to drive to the room we had been monitoring.

I asked her, "Is anyone inside?"

"No," she replied, looking away.

Knowing there were at least one male and one female inside, I suspected it could be a set up to rip me off, which is not uncommon. Johns are easy targets for robberies because most won't report the incident to the police. As we got closer to the room, the team intercepted us. The pimp and the girls were all from the Los Angeles area. We arrested the pimp, who wore a probation ankle monitor.

I called Debra to assist with talking to the women to try and get them to accept our services. I wondered if she would measure up. What I witnessed led me to believe Debra was the right person in the right place for such a time as this.

Debra related to the women in a way none of us could have. She had walked in their shoes, which gave her credibility.

What happened at Breaking the Chains was simply amazing and something I had never seen before. Within a year after I met Debra, her efforts led to a long-term safe house with wrap-around services, built from private donations. The house quickly filled with clients, and services are offered to many more. Debra's success showed a community and those directly involved how quickly something can be done without government funding. It took Debra, someone who lived and survived the pain, to help us understand you can't label a woman because of her lifestyle. They have hearts and stories, and we can open our arms to embrace and love them.

I am proud to help Debra and Tiffany continue to do what they unselfishly do for others. It all works together: education on all fronts—law enforcement, the community, a change in the laws, and support services for victims. Together, we measure our success by those who are no longer tormented by the life they were once forced to live and by the offenders who are held accountable to a level they've never been held to before. Lives change with an ongoing network of services provided.

Together, we are breaking the chains, one victim at a time.

ACKNOWLEDGEMENTS

Debra Rush
The story of redemption and unconditional love is best played out through the story of the cross. Although my own story pales in comparison to that of our Risen Savior, I cannot help but see His reflection in every moment of my life. In looking back, I can clearly see His strong arms holding me and His perfect plan for my life unfolding in every teardrop.

In writing this book, there are so many people that God used to lift me up, strengthen me, give me wisdom, and direct me to the place I stand today. For them, I am eternally grateful. Yet there are those individuals whose impact has been so tremendous I could not even imagine my life without them. God has blessed me and Breaking the Chains with wonderful friends and supporters. In these pages, I pray they know that they are loved and that my gratitude is unending.

First and foremost, to my husband Mark. You are an incredible blessing from God. Thank you for your unconditional love and ability to completely overlook all the stains of my past. You are a picture of Christ's love for the church in its purest form. You are the answer to my prayer at the beginning of the book, and I have no doubt that I was created for you before the foundations of this earth were laid. Your love and adoration remind me every single day that no one, not even a girl with my past, is beyond redemption. God's plans always prevail.

God gave me the most incredible family, my children, who have walked with me since birth through the worst of times. I am so proud to be your mom. Mark gifted me with three more wonderful kids through our marriage, and now we are nine. My life is full beyond my imagination.

To Daddy, you are the best father a girl can imagine. Without your unfailing love throughout my life, I would never have made it.

I have been blessed to have so many hands guide me to where I am today; Sharon Hoard, who invested many hours to providing guidance, The New Beginnings Church members welcomed me with open arms at a time I needed to be accepted. Thank you to the person who paid my way to Pinecrest where God spoke to me. Tom Sommers, who encouraged me to start Breaking the Chains, even when I had no self-confidence. I am thankful for his generous gift of time and for introducing me to people who could help.

I will be eternally grateful to law enforcement, starting with Detective Fries, who saw beyond the tough girl on the street. Chief Jerry Dyer, who agreed to speak at Breaking the Chains' first banquet and now serves on the board. Since the day I met him, Chief Dyer has always been a source of support, advice, and encouragement. Sergeant Curtis Chastain, head of the Human Trafficking Division, who supports Breaking the Chains totally. He was one of the first who clearly saw the need for a special program for women on the streets.

To Tiffany Apodaca, God had you in mind when He picked you as my partner and co-founder. I am grateful every day for your presence in my life, always by my side and often the cooler head.

To Penny Childers, I am honored and humbled that you chose my story as your debut book. You've been patient and diligent in making sure that the story came out just right. Without you, the story may never have been told. I love you, and I simply cannot thank you enough.

To my grandmother, whose arms were always my place of refuge. When I was with her, I felt her strong, unshakeable love. Her words were saturated with God's wisdom. Grandma nurtured me from birth, until she took her final breath, when I was twenty-three years old. Grandma never saw me as who I am today, but she knew I would make it. Her prayers and promises are still inside my heart and continue to guide me. She built me up and helped to mold the mountain-moving faith that I have to this very day.

Finally, I am grateful to my mother for bringing me into the world—for choosing life for me. The sweet moments of closeness we had together, as she lay on her deathbed, will forever bring me comfort.

Penelope Childers

In the fall of 2014, I met Debra Woods and Tiffany Apodaca at a coffee shop to discuss the specifics of a banquet they were planning for their organization. Not knowing who they were or what they represented, I agreed to meet with them as a favor to a friend. It was quite a surprise to learn that they were co-founders of Breaking the Chains, an organization dedicated to rescuing and rehabilitating victims of sex trafficking.

When Debra revealed, she was once a victim herself, I was in awe. I had never personally known someone who had such an experience. When Debra asked me to write her story, I told her I would get back to her early the next year but never did. A few months later, I met her again. She gently confronted me. "I thought you were going to get back to me. I was sure God told me you were the one to write my book."

I told her again I would call her early the next year. I called her a few months later and asked, "Are you ready?"

The journey that Debra and I have shared has been life-changing. Debra found it difficult to tell me many details of her past. Details she'd never told anyone. Over the many months, I spent with Debra, my perception of women on the streets changed from one of indifference and judgment to one of understanding and empathy. I am deeply honored that Debra chose me to be her co-author and will be forever grateful for her trust in me to write her deeply personal story.

I have many people to thank, starting with my husband Larry, who encouraged me and allowed me to spend many hours writing this book. Thank you to my daughter, Megan Pascual, who answered questions about court proceedings and supported me without fail. Thank you to my friend, Officer Mike Kirby, who always responded to questions I had regarding police procedures.

No one writes a book, or at least their first book, without the support of a tribe. I indeed have one. Thank you to my Tuesday writers' critique group, whose honest feedback kept me on track: Vicki Caine, our leader, who never failed to help me when I asked, and Barbara Capell, who opened her home every week to our writing group: Nancy Wright, Jeannie Kowalczyk, Lousia Weyant, Tuly Michailides, Phyllis Brown, and Martha Tessmer. Thank you to my friend, Charlotte Rickles, who met with me from the time I started writing and stayed with me till the end. Her teaching and mentoring skills were a gift that I cannot repay. Thank you to those who read for me: Cathy Grant, Kelly Wendell Janneck, San Dee Rooney, Linda Lochridge Hoenigsberg, and Vicki DeLeon. Your insights were extremely helpful. Thank you to my good friend Donna Waller; her editing skills put the final changes in the manuscript. And to Annette Sherian, Sharon Sheppard, and Teri Sherron for their encouragement and sharp eyes in finding those last tiny little errors.

I cannot forget to mention those special authors I met at Mount Hermon Christian Writers Conference, who never failed to mentor and encourage me just when I needed it. A special thank you to my dear friend and author, Susan Mustafa, whom I've never met, but her gifts of encouragement, phone conversations, and time were more valuable than she will ever know.

Readers, thank you for taking the time to read *A Cry of the Heart*. It is my hope that in some small way Debra's story has touched your heart, opened your eyes, and brought you healing.

♦ ♦ ♦

We are grateful to each one who believed in this project and provided financial support; Darrius Assemi, Debbie and Charles Dorkensen.

Photograph credit: Jamie Ouverson and Ken Scheid.

HELP ME!

Know the Red Flags of a Sex Traffic Victim

- Evidence of being controlled
- Not free to leave or come and go as she/he wishes
- Responds with rehearsed answers
- Lacks control of earned money or identification
- Avoids eye contact
- Defensive or argumentative
- Mistrust of individuals displaying compassion
- Bonded with her/his abuser, despite physical or sexual violence
- Tattoos or scarring of trafficker's name and/or symbols on the victim's body
- Visible signs of sexual violence, physical restraint, confinement, or torture
- Malnourished, exhausted, sleep deprived
- Poor hygiene

If you suspect someone is being trafficked, contact 1-888-373-7888
Resource: YWCA

DISCUSSION QUESTIONS

1) What surprised you the most about Debra's story? Why?
2) What, if anything, were you able to relate to?
3) On Christmas night, Debra found herself alone in a jail holding cell. When she made a call to her father for help, he told her that he loved her but would no longer rescue her. God was her only hope now. Have you ever found yourself in a similar situation? What did you do? What was the result?
4) How did you see God bring people into Debra's life who helped move her toward her future?
5) What did God want Mrs. Hoard to do? How might things be different if she had been disobedient? For Debra? For Mrs. Hoard? Has God ever asked you to do something you didn't want to do? What was your response? What was the result?
6) What most spoke to you about this story? Why?
7) How did you see post-traumatic stress (PTS) manifest itself through the eight years after Debra escaped? Looking back over your life, have you ever experienced PTS?
8) What events took place, simultaneously, that would eventually intersect for good and the fight against sex trafficking?
9) Debra's story is a life-changing story for herself, her children, her friends on the street, and those she touches along the way. Was there anything in this story life-changing for you? If so, what?

BREAKING THE CHAINS

Providing Healing and Restoration to Survivors of Human Trafficking

Debra Rush
Co-Founder/CEO

For more information on Breaking the Chains or to book Debra for a speaking engagement visit:

www.btcfresno.org
Facebook page: Debra Rush

Debra Rush is a co-founder and the Chief Executive Officer of Breaking the Chains. Debra's insight and experience into this dauntless industry is the driving force in which Breaking the Chains was founded. Debra is a survivor of human trafficking. In 1999, she was rescued and taken to a confidential location, which isolated her from the region where she was held captive. Unfortunately, at that time, no efforts were being made to expose human trafficking, and there were limited resources available to help her cope with the specific trauma she had endured. In 2008, after years of guilt and shame, she found the courage and strength to begin her healing journey. This spurred her quest to rescue women who are trapped in human trafficking and believe there is no way out. In the spring of 2014, Debra Rush and Tiffany Apodaca partnered to build the Central Valley's first adult safe house, which is currently helping women escape systems of sexual exploitation through advocacy, direct services, housing, and education. Debra has a degree in Human Services and extensive experience as an Alcohol and Drug Counselor. She is happily married and enjoys spending time with her family. In 2018, Debra was named State of California Woman of the Year.

Penelope Childers began writing in 2010 and has published short stories in several magazines. *A Cry of the Heart* is her first completed collative writing project. Penelope has a heart for writing stories that inspire, transform, and help readers to heal from life's trauma.

57183177R00121

Made in the USA
Columbia, SC
06 May 2019